GIRLS DON'T RIDE MOTORBIKES

A Spiritual Adventure Into Life's Labyrinth

May the light always
Shine on your
path , Dorit

DORIT BRAUER

ISBN: 1470026198
ISBN 13: 9781470026196

11-circuit Chartres Labyrinth

7-circuit Labyrinth

TABLE OF CONTENTS

PROLOGUE

One

I am not the hawk soaring high up in the sky, above all.
I am not the purple cactus, different and standing all alone.
I am not the humming bee, ready to sting when you come too close.

I am the single drop of water listening to the call.
I dare to jump and plunge into the pond.
A commotion stirs the surface, waves spread in circles all around.

THE AWAKENING

My life was comfortable, filled with pleasant predictable routines. I had lived in the same area for six years and built a successful career in holistic health. For the first time I was financially secure and envisioned settling down, buying a house and opening my own healing practice.

The part of me that had rested quietly for many years woke up one day, shortly after I turned thirty-eight. At first, it chatted gently, slowly awakening from a deep sleep, lazy and yawning. It teased me, playfully reminded me that life is large, that there is more to explore. I knew this part of my personality so well. It demanded change. I tried to ignore the force that yet again would push me forward.

"The life you live now is not it," this part of me said. "It's only one little identification of yours."

"You call this a little identification?" I argued back. "Everything I do is really important to me."

"Exactly. You are getting too attached." The inner voice grew stronger. "There is more to life. Rethink where you are going."

Attentively, I considered my options. With my upcoming fortieth birthday, I could plan a trip – maybe revisit Brazil and retrace where a different journey many years ago had begun. I picked up a *Lonely Planet Handbook* and leafed through the pages. Colorful pictures showed familiar sights: Rio de Janeiro, Foz de Iguaçu, the capital Brasília, the Amazon River, the dunes of Fortaleza. I recalled the half-dozen times I slept outdoors on secluded beaches, drifting to sleep while gazing at an endless star-filled sky and listening to rolling waves. Far from civilization, nature had provided the positive benefit of saving money. Once in Manaus, the night before my passage down the Amazon, I stayed in the cheapest hotel at the fish harbor. Cockroaches infested the shabby room and the ugly creatures tap-danced up and down the walls all night long. I buried my head beneath the sheets, trying to get some rest.

I flipped to the page that listed the required vaccinations against malaria, typhoid and yellow fever. 'Do I really want to go through this again?' I wondered.

'I am older now and this is not my way of travel any longer. Why retrace the past?' This thought kept spinning inside my head. A couple of weeks later, my passion for motorcycles and travel and the fascination with sacred circles combined and led me to the idea of a cross-country motorcycle road trip to walk labyrinths. The day I hung a map of the United States on my office wall and traced my itinerary with a yellow marker, the inner dialogue ceased. I knew that my destiny called me to get on the road and breathe in the world. And while traveling forward on my journey, I would have plenty of time to reflect on how I got here.

1

Pittsburgh. Monday, August 14, 2006. The alarm rang at 6:00 a.m. I awoke, eager to start the day, got out of bed, and pulled on my black leather pants. Worn from riding, they bulged at the knees. Too much sun had turned the color on the upper legs to a soft earthy brown. The smooth leather emitted a delicious scent of adventure and protectively wrapped around my legs. I threw on a light green T-shirt and pulled my shoulder length brown hair back into a ponytail. I slipped on a silver necklace, a gift for my journey from my boyfriend, Frank. Its three brilliant crystals reflected the sunlight in sparkling rays of rainbow colors.

I opened the bedroom window. The fresh morning air tickled my skin. Cheerful singing birds invited the new day. From my elevated perspective on the top of a hill, I saw the red roof of my landlord's house. The clear water of a bright turquoise swimming pool shimmered in the rising morning sun. Planters on the wooden deck overflowed with crimson, white and purple petunias. Tall sycamores, showing off their distinctive creamy white bark, graceful elms, silver maples, attractive locusts and abundant walnut trees surrounded the home.

'This is a good place to live,' I thought, and a sad ache permeated my heart. 'I could stay here. I don't have to leave.' The inner dialogue persisted.

"Dorit, come on," Frank called. "It's time to go." He threw me a kiss with a boyish twinkle in his blue eyes and then took my bags. I watched the fluid movement of his tall and slender body. I adored his handsome face, his straight beautiful nose, his high forehead, even his receding hairline. Frank

1

was easygoing. He felt comfortable with himself, was always confident and present. He loved the outdoors and his profession as a tree climber and arborist.

Wearing heavy biker boots, I grabbed my jacket and helmet. One last time I glanced at the silver frame that held a picture of my father. He rode my silver-grey mare, Estella, wearing a white shirt, black pants and leather boots. He was a tall, handsome man with broad shoulders, dark black hair, a full beard and a nose distinctively shaped like a hawk's beak. His tough hands held the reins and my horse obeyed. She bent her neck with discipline. The picture had been taken on the green fertile land of our family farm in the Lower Rhine Valley of Germany. Wild chestnut trees stood tall and straight in the background, a clear metaphor for a strict upbringing. My father's bright green eyes did not look into the camera but rather at a far point in the distance. He smiled contentedly.

A cold shiver stopped me as I walked down the stairs. For a moment, I felt my father's presence. He tugged my right shoulder back, and his warning voice whispered into my ear, "Girls don't ride motorbikes." I shook him off and hurried to the garage.

Frank was busy strapping the luggage onto my blue Suzuki Bandit 600. Two saddlebags and one tour bag held the bare necessities for the six-week trip. I strapped on the tank bag, held by magnets on top of the fuel tank. It held my maps, a camera, a recording device, a picture of a labyrinth and a St. Christopher medallion, the protective saint of travelers. I zipped the card I had received from my mom into a separate compartment. It read: 'Dear Dorit, I send my best wishes to you for a good journey. I wish you joy, equal to the infinite number of drops in a refreshing morning rain, and fortune that equals the number of stars in the sky. I wish you love as much as the sun has rays. And when you stand up high on a mountain road, close to the heavens, remember that your family loves you and your father is watching over you from the other side. Love, Mom.'

Frank started his silver Yamaha FZ 1. The engine howled, then quickly settled into a steady hum. I switched the starter on my bike and the garage filled with the idling rhythm of two powerful machines. The sound was music to my ears. Then I tried to push my bike off its center stand. I had done this many times, but it did not move.

"Frank," I asked, "can you help me?" He had backed his motorcycle outside, ready to go.

My bike was too heavy. Fully loaded, it weighed more than 520 pounds. "Could you hold it while I push it off its stand so that it doesn't fall over?" I asked.

Forcefully, I pushed the bike forward off its center; it wobbled left and right as Frank balanced it.

I quickly released the side stand with one foot and leaned the bike to the left to a stable and safe position.

"Wow, this is serious," I said. "How can I do this by myself? The bike needs to be on the center stand when I pack it so that the luggage is balanced."

"Let's try again," Frank suggested with an optimistic smile.

Together we heaved the bike back onto its center stand. Then I pushed it forward with all my strength. It swayed dangerously and Frank forced it straight. The next time, I positioned myself closer to the bike's middle and noticed that I had more control. Two attempts later, I was exhausted and my arms were shaking from the effort, but I felt confident that I could master the delicate balancing act.

"Well, I guess I can always ask for help," I concluded.

I put on my well-worn leather gloves and the full-face helmet, then got onto my machine, opened the throttle and drove off without looking back. I rode with care, adjusting to the additional weight. Frank rode next to me. He recognized that I was comfortably gaining speed and gave me the thumbs up. I nodded.

Shortly after 7:00 a.m., we arrived at Westminster Presbyterian Church in Pittsburgh. Eleven friends were waiting. Most of the nine women and two men had previously attended my meditation classes. I felt grateful that they all joined me for a labyrinth walk.

The Courtyard of Spirit, rich with lush green trees, and the warm terracotta labyrinth invited us in. The labyrinth was laid out in the ground with red and ochre stones creating a 28-foot complex spiral circle. I asked my friends to gather within its perimeter. We held hands.

"Thank you for being here this morning," I said. "Let's all connect together before we embark on our journey into the labyrinth."

"This pattern looks complicated; is there anything I can do wrong when I walk it?" my friend Maureen asked.

"No, it's easy. The labyrinth is a one-way path that will automatically lead you to the center. You can't get lost, and once you have reached the center you follow the same path out. Just put one foot in front of the other and trust yourself," I responded.

Maureen nodded. Then we all closed our eyes, took deep breaths and stood in silence for a few moments.

Wind rustled in the trees. A single bird chirped, and the sounds of passing cars echoed into the courtyard. Several minutes later we opened our eyes. I suggested that during the walk we could focus on our breathing. "Let's visualize inhaling bright-shining, benevolent light and exhaling everything we wish to release," I advised. "Eventually, we will be entirely filled with light, and it will grow, expand and intensify all around."

I watched my friends as they entered the labyrinth. To my left was the courtyard. Flowers, placed for deceased loved ones, slowly withered away. Their heavy fragrance saturated the air. I stood across from a bronze statue of a praying maiden, who bowed her head, and I was amazed at how easily the words "God" and "The Divine" rolled off my tongue.

For the greater part of my life these words had never crossed my lips. I had grown up in a reasonably devout Catholic household. My mom went to church on Sunday and lit candles for everyone in need of God's special intervention. After I had left home at nineteen, she pointed out that most candles were being lit for me, the cause of her sleepless nights.

My dad had entered the house of God only on Christmas and Easter, and for weddings, funerals and the annual village celebration, the Schützenfest. He rode on horseback in a parade to church, dressed in a viridian green uniform, heavily decorated with shiny Schützenfest medals, which were attained over the course of many years by shooting off parts of a wooden bird. The red and white feathers on his hat waved in the wind. Then following the service, the entire village turned into one big drinking festival.

My brother Jörg and I sided with our dad and whined about going to church. That's when our mom had the brilliant idea to bribe us. I was around eight at the time. Before church, we would negotiate the terms: two or three scoops of ice cream, with whipped cream or not, or cake from the best baker in town.

At fourteen I opted not to attend religious classes in school and did not find it necessary to tell my parents. In Germany, at fourteen, students can choose not to study religion. At my school nobody had ever taken advantage of this law. Only two other kids and I were brave enough not to conform.

The director, appalled by our decision, gave us chores. Two hours per week, when the good kids studied the bible, the three of us, large brooms in our hands, swept the schoolyard.

My skepticism about organized religion grew as I became older. For me, if there were a God, this force dwelled in places other than church.

The shift in my consciousness happened in my mid-thirties, during the four years I taught meditation at the University of Pittsburgh Medical Center. Conveniently, in the scientific environment, the mention of God is frowned upon, as God is the opposite of science.

However, to me, science does not offer all the answers. A brain can be dissected into its smallest components in order to examine how everything works. But the question *why* is an unanswered mystery. Why does a brain cell know to become a brain cell and not a liver or kidney cell? And maybe our brain is only the receiver of an invisible higher force.

During meditation I have experienced myself beyond the confinement of the physical. I describe this state of mind as connecting to the universe, a superior power, the light, your supreme being. I could not deny what was becoming obvious. I felt that all of creation is called into existence by one force which moves everything: God.

When I finally decided to leave the halls of science and ventured on to open my own business, I recorded a new meditation CD for my students called *Open your heart and receive God's love*.

I sent my mom a copy and she phoned immediately.

"The dictionary translates God into Gott (God in German)," she said.

"Yes, mom."

She was quiet for a moment, and then she asked, emphasizing every single word, "You believe in God?"

"Well, it has been a long evolution, but I really feel there is only one force that creates everything; we might as well call it God."

From across the ocean, I heard a sigh of relief and assumed that my mom was delighted that her prayers finally had come to fruition.

I was the last one to step into the labyrinth and together with my friends walked in silence, as we circled deeper toward the center. At first, heaviness burdened the field. After everyone reached the middle, and then one by one retraced their way out of the labyrinth, joy spread through me like a wave and I felt embraced by a universal smile. In our closing ceremony, I suggested that we send the divine light from our hearts into the world and visualize it spreading to all directions without limits.

My friend Maureen spoke first, "I was able to let go of all my worries. There is so much peace. It's incredible. I feel relaxed, energized and free at the same time."

"That's great," I said. "The challenge, of course, is to maintain this feeling in everyday life, but the more you walk labyrinths or meditate, the easier it becomes. It's just a matter of practice. Just like physical exercise. The more you practice, the better you get."

Punctually, at 8:00 a.m., I pulled out of the church parking lot; my friends waved their goodbyes. The earlier melancholy of leaving home was replaced by an all-absorbing anticipation of adventure. Frank rode next to me. He joined me for the first 100 miles of the journey. We left the congested morning traffic behind and got onto I-79, traveling south. I checked my speedometer and noticed that I was exceeding the allowed speed limit. I mused about the pleasure of driving at unbounded speed on the German Autobahn, while I carefully hit the rear brake and slowed down. 'This is America,' I reminded myself.

Riding a motorcycle is one of life's greatest pleasures. I love the freedom to be present in the here and now and all alone.

I love the joy of focused attention required to handle the machine or the intimate balance as I shift my weight and lean the bike into a curve. My soul thoroughly anchors in the body for every movement. The right hand turns the throttle. It also operates the front brakes. My right foot handles the rear brake. My left hand pulls the clutch lever and simultaneously the left foot controls the gear shifter. Riding is bliss.

My face in the wind, I ride from sun to shade to sun, and the shifts in temperature tickle my skin. I enjoy my greatest moments of reflection and introspection when I ride on empty country roads. A mesmerizing extension of perception allows me to concentrate on the physical demands of operating this perfect machine, and at the same time, I send my awareness out ahead to scan the road for obstacles. My highly trained sixth sense often receives the clear message to slow down before coming around a turn. Sometimes a deer crosses or a fallen tree branch blocks the lane. In high traffic, I experience the elevated psychic perception of knowing in advance the sudden move of a driver. It has kept me safe, amazing me anew each time, reconfirming the infinite abilities of the human mind.

We turned onto I-70 heading toward West Virginia. The Wheeling tunnel took us in. Moments later the tight, dark passageway released us onto the arched Fort Henry Bridge crossing the Ohio River. The river current reflected the bright morning light. My body instantly relaxed and breathing space filled my chest. A carefree lightness uplifted me.

Developed from my many strolls along the River Rhine during my youth on the dairy farm in Germany, this mystifying reaction of my body to the sight of a river has proven itself useful during times of stress. I couldn't count the number of motorcycle rides I have taken along the Ohio River throughout the past years. I have been able to create an equally positive response by simply imagining a river.

Through Bridgeport we continued onto the two-lane Route 7, which parallels the river. The sky was blue, the land rich and green. The river meandered peacefully, occasionally revealing a barge carrying coal. We passed through deserted towns with only a handful of people and cars. At the 100-mile mark, we entered the sleepy little town of Sardis and found a restaurant open for breakfast. Frank and I were the only customers. We filled our bellies with tasty pancakes, bacon and eggs, coffee and orange juice. Then it was time to go.

Not fond of long goodbyes, I gave Frank a quick hug, ready to get on my bike. But he held me tight and wrapped his arms around me. I inhaled the scent of his warm skin. He kissed my neck, my face and then my lips. A pleasant familiar shiver ran down my spine.

"I love you," he said with his sweet voice.

"I love you, too," I whispered and thought how nice it would be if this love would never end. I loosened myself from his grip, gave him one last kiss and put on my helmet.

Side by side we rode back to the main road. Frank turned right and I turned left. I watched him disappear in my bike's mirror. Then alone, I focused on the road ahead.

2

I chose to take the scenic road instead of the faster highway. 'Following the river was the appropriate analogy for my journey,' I thought. I saw the river as a symbol of my ability to go with the flow of life and change. Nothing was ever the same. I could step into the river with one foot, and by the time the second foot reached the water, the river would already be completely new.

On the surface, reality may appear the same each day, but in essence, we are new every moment of our lives. The potential for change and growth is unlimited if we allow ourselves to surrender to the flow of life.

Suddenly a grinding clack, clack, clack jolted me out of my thoughts. The engine choked. I hadn't paid attention to the fuel level. I turned the reserve lever for additional gas. The machine recovered to its steady pleasant hum. Not worried, I continued my ride on the lonely country road as it ran close to the river. Abundant fields of corn and wheat promised a rich harvest. I was falling in love with the endless groves of wild untamed oaks, elms, maples and sycamores; opulent solid undergrowth immediately covered fallen branches and trees.

In comparison, German forests and tree groves are rigorously domesticated, the underbrush cleaned away and the trees tall and straight like disciplined soldiers, with no room for anything truly wild.

Ten miles later, I reached a fuel station. Two lonely pumps stood in quiet desperation, their coat of once bright color peeled off, leaving a dirty brownish white. My heart sank; diesel and regular were being sold but not high octane 93 fuel. My precious sport touring bike consumes premium fuel, and I did not intend to fill it up with inferior quality. A quick calculation convinced me that the reserve fuel might last for another 20 miles. If I was lucky, 25.

I entered the small store and was pushed back by the sticky, hot air. The ceiling fan whizzed with futile effort. Half-empty shelves displayed life's essentials: laundry detergent, toilet paper and sugar. The fridge contained gallon containers of milk and red cans of coke but no bottled water.

I asked the clerk, "How far is it to the next fuel station?"

He frowned. "Ah, 'bout 20 miles." He was a weathered man in his fifties. A green baseball cap with a yellow John Deere tractor logo covered his brown hair. A cigarette was stuck behind his left ear. He wore a black, red and white checkered shirt and his washed-out jeans were covered with oil stains. He turned his head and looked out the window at my bike.

"That's yours?" he asked.

"Yes."

"Where're you going?"

"Out West, to California."

He shook his head and looked at me in disbelief. "Long ways to go," he said.

I walked to the entrance door. "Yes, that's true. Well, thank you and have a nice day."

"Be safe. It's dangerous out there," he cautioned.

I shrugged my shoulders and got on my bike.

The ride continued on deserted country roads. I enjoyed being by myself. The half-open visor allowed the wind to stream onto my face. The bike ran smoothly through long elegant curves. The clerk's words "It's dangerous out there" stayed in my brain. My studies in mysticism had taught me that the outside world is a reflection of the inside world. In psychology, it is called projection. Consequently, the real danger is within us. Personally, I consider staying at home more dangerous than daring to venture out and explore.

I vividly recalled the moment of this realization, the pivotal point in my life. My best friend Silke had died at fifteen of lung cancer. We had grown up on neighboring farms; both owned horses and enjoyed spending long afternoons riding together. The disease had taken her suddenly and quickly.

Returning from the funeral, my father and I stood outside, overlooking our farm's meadows. The day was crisp and sad. My eyes were sore from crying. I felt weak and wondered how this could have happened. Silke was too young to die.

"Dad, where is Silke now?" I asked. "What happens after we die? Is there a continuation after death?"

"No," he said. "There is nothing after death."

"But Dad, that doesn't make sense."

"There is nothing," he said with a controlled tone in his voice, implying that I should not dare ask another question. I looked into my father's green eyes and for the first time I recognized emotions I had never seen in him: resignation, defeat and fear.

We stood in silence. My horse grazed in the meadow next to the levy. The River Rhine flowed leisurely toward the North Sea. My entire being ached. Silke and I had loved to race our horses. We galloped at high speed along the river, our hair flying in the wind. After harvest time, expansive open stubble fields invited us for a contest. My horse Estella always won. She was faster than Silke's pretty brown mare. A few times we raced head to head, but I always pressed Estella forward to finish first. My competitiveness had filled me with pride then, but it was the cause of regret after Silke's death. The thought that I should have pushed my horse less so that Silke would have won tore me apart.

Steel grey clouds weighed heavily. I looked up and knew that beyond the clouds were a wide open sky and a bright, shining, warm sun. Visible or not, it was a certainty. As if in response to my thoughts, the sky opened on the other side across the River Rhine and a single ray of sunlight illuminated the earth. I had turned away from my dad and never asked again.

That same afternoon, I pedaled my bicycle the few miles to town. Out of breath, my eyes still red from crying, I arrived at the library shortly before 3:00 pm. The librarian had just returned from his break and unlocked the door. He was a tall lanky man in his thirties with thick-rimmed glasses and wild black hair.

"Do you have any books about life after death?" I asked.

"Yes," he said and nodded. He knew the reason for my question. In our small town everybody was touched by the death of the young teenage girl.

I followed him up the stairs to the second floor. We walked past the shelves marked for religious studies into the psychology section. He picked two books for me, *On Death and Dying* by Elisabeth Kübler-Ross and *Life after Life* by Raymond Moody.

"Are there any books about rein-carnation?" I asked, not quite sure how to pronounce the word that I had discovered in an article about Eastern philosophy.

"You mean re-incarnation?" he asked.

"Yes, that's it, re-incarnation."

He pulled a yellow hardcover book from an upper shelf. The title read *Twenty Cases Suggestive of Reincarnation* by Dr. Ian Stevenson.

I read the three books in one week. They opened my mind to a deeper understanding of who we are as human beings. *On Death and Dying* by Elisabeth Kübler-Ross, a Swiss born psychiatrist, who had researched patients diagnosed with terminal illness, described the five stages of grief that people go through when facing their own deaths. The second book was *Life after Life* by Raymond Moody, a psychologist with a medical degree, who had investigated more than one hundred case studies of people who had experienced clinical death and had been revived.

The third book *Twenty Cases Suggestive of Reincarnation* had been written by Ian Stevenson, the head of the Department of Psychiatry at the University of Virginia. Dr. Stevenson had investigated cases of children who claimed to remember a past life. This book took me even further. I recalled a number of dreams in which I had seen myself in different bodies, places and times. I wondered if these were memories of other life times. I realized that my dreams may have been actual experiences and not pure fabrication of my vivid imagination. I was curious and wanted to learn more. My inquiries had pointed the way to self-discovery.

The day Silke died I became a seeker.

The urge to find answers led me to leave home, to travel, to explore the unknown and to study with a variety of metaphysical teachers. At age forty, I knew that for me it was safer to choose the dangerous route.

The next fuel station was closed. I took a deep breath and rode on. I considered the irony of getting stranded the first day of my trip. I drove another ten miles. The brilliant cerulean sky disappeared behind towering white cumulus clouds. Then the engine coughed in a demand for gasoline. A small village came into sight and a sign indicated a service station. Relieved, I pulled in as my bike choked and rebelled on its last drops. Only diesel and regular were for sale. I took out my map to calculate the distance to Cincinnati. I had no choice and filled the tank halfway with regular fuel.

A light drizzle started. I put on my rain gear and drove off. The rain played a rhythmic staccato on my helmet. I inhaled the delightful scent of the earth, intensified by the moist air. I took pleasure in the expansive ripe green of the grass, the rich invigorating fragrance of freshly plowed land and the distinctive rich aroma of cow pastures. In Cincinnati I filled my tank with high octane fuel and then merged onto I-71 to Louisville, Kentucky.

3

At 7:00 p.m., I arrived at the Presbyterian Seminary in Louisville, Kentucky. Their labyrinth is surrounded by a park of trees and lawns on a Victorian estate. I rode 515 miles on my first day. I parked the bike close to the 66-foot, 11-circuit grass labyrinth and walked to a wooden bench, sat down and freed my feet from the heavy biker boots. The rain had stopped and I peeled myself out of my gear. In my leather pants and T-shirt, I was light and free.

I closed my eyes and saw my arrival at this labyrinth a year earlier when I had participated in the labyrinth facilitator training with Dr. Lauren Artress, the author of *Walking a Sacred Path - Rediscovering the Labyrinth as a Spiritual Tool*. Dr. Artress had traveled to the Chartres Cathedral in France, copied the design of the labyrinth embedded in the nave of the cathedral and taken it to Grace Cathedral in San Francisco.

A year ago, I sat on a bench and admired the magnificence and precision of Louisville's sacred circle. A tall woman in her sixties tended the flowers. Carefully her rubber-gloved hands navigated a rake around the yellow and red chrysanthemums. The setting sun surrounded her with an aura of soft light. I took deep breaths, centered myself and walked clockwise around the labyrinth's perimeter. I reached the woman and paused.

"The flowers are beautiful," I said.

She lifted her head. Her face was fine and relaxed; her brown eyes carried the depth and knowledge of a fulfilled life.

"Thank you," she said. "Are you here for the retreat?"

"Yes."

"I am Rebecca Smith Ritchey, a spiritual director at the Seminary. Enjoy your labyrinth walk. It is wonderful that you are here."

She smiled and focused her attention back to the flowers. Then I walked the labyrinth. I took slow deliberate steps for the hour it took to complete my journey. I had never experienced a grass labyrinth and treasured the sensual connection to Mother Earth.

I opened my eyes and returned to the present moment after having reveled in memories. I saw my motorcycle nearby. I was the only person here. The sky was calm and covered with a thin sheet of grey clouds. Like a layer of silk, it allowed tender rays of sun to shine through.

I marveled at the mystery of the labyrinth's origin. The 11-circuit labyrinth in the Chartres Cathedral near Paris, France, had most likely been built during the second decade of the 13th century, around 1215-1221. The design of the labyrinth at Chartres was widespread in Europe from the 11th century onward, and a number of examples of this style were placed in churches and cathedrals in Italy during the 12th century. The design had originated amongst the scholars and scribes creating manuscripts in monasteries in Europe, probably during the 10th century.

I have heard of highly speculative claims linking the circular labyrinth design to the Knights Templar, who may have brought it from the Holy Land and King Solomon's Temple directly to France, or to the Freemasons, the builders of the Gothic cathedrals in Europe.

No matter from where they came, I have experienced labyrinths as a gift from a forgotten past when body and mind were not separated. During the 15th century, with the introduction of rationalism, the perception of reality had moved away from the intuitive, non-linear, and mystical toward the scientific and logical understanding of the world. Throughout the next 200 years, the labyrinths in Europe's great cathedrals were destroyed. During the same time period tens of thousands of women, accused of witchcraft, were burned alive at the stake in Europe. Things unexplainable and mysterious were demonized. To me, the labyrinth invites us to reconnect with the deeply intuitive and creative parts of ourselves, the round, feminine and non-linear.

I reached into the pocket of my motorcycle jacket for the rosary, a gift from my friend Daria. The red prayer beads ran through my fingers. The wood was smooth, soft and saturated with the sweet perfume of roses. Never before had I prayed with a rosary. I counted five groups of ten beads with single ones in between.

I stepped toward the labyrinth's entrance, bowed and slowly moved forward. I focused my thoughts on gratitude as the prayer beads slipped through my fingers. There was so much to appreciate and to be grateful for. I remembered Daria's words when she had handed me the rosary. "This rosary will bring a miracle," she said.

I recalled Einstein's words. Einstein said that there are only two ways to view life, either as if nothing is a miracle or as if everything is a miracle.

The labyrinth took me in like a warm, nurturing and all-providing womb. Red terracotta bricks marked the meandering path in the grass. The earth was moist and smooth, a living breathing being. My bare feet connected me to its soul. With every step, it felt as if the soles of my feet were making love to the soil. In joyful celebration, the spirited orgasmic energy traveled from my toes to the top of my head. The intensity of this enchanting journey grew. My entire body rejoiced with intoxicating ecstasy. The thoughts inside my head began to spin. 'Yes, yes, yes.' The earth's energy forcefully pulsed up my spine, and I feared my head would burst open and my spirit would break loose and soar away. I never before had known that I could have an orgasm with earth. I felt I needed to slow down and began to focus on the rosary and counted the beads aloud, "One, two, three, four, five, six, seven, eight, nine, ten. One. One, two, three, four, five." I synchronized my footsteps to my words and followed the path through the endless twists and turns.

I circled through the four equal quarters and changed directions at twenty-eight 180 degree turns and six semi-right-angle turns. Lightheaded, I entered the spacious center of the labyrinth. A prickling sensation turned my skin into goose bumps, as if caressed by a light breeze. But there was no wind and the still silver sky watched silently. Standing in the middle, I admired the path that had led me here. It looked similar to the intertwining loops of a brain. Once I heard someone say, "Our head is round so that our thoughts can change directions."

In deep reflection, I followed the one-way path out of the labyrinth. The smooth red prayer beads of the rosary ran through my fingers. The sky opened and sunrays shone on me. The leaves of trees rustled in unison rhythm, synchronous with the in and out breath of the earth. Birds sang. I felt like dancing and leaped forward with fast, light steps, feeling I was one with nature and one with the universe.

Then I got on my bike and followed the directions to Rebecca's house. She had generously invited me to stay for two nights. A year had passed since we first met and I was happy to see her. We relaxed on her porch. Fragrant flowers surrounded us. Hummingbirds hovered in midair rapidly flapping their wings. The evening light turned the world soft and mellow.

"I love walking labyrinths," I said. "I learn something new every time. My life has become so rich."

"Yes, I agree," Rebecca smiled. "You are very devoted and I feel exactly the same way. I have been a devotee since my very first labyrinth experience," she continued. "Actually my most incredible labyrinth experience took place at the Kordes Retreat Center in Ferdinand, Indiana. I'll get the brochure. It's on your way, only 60 miles west of Louisville. You should stop there." Rebecca went into the house and returned with a leaflet. It showed the impressive red brick Monastery Immaculate Conception, home of the Sisters of St. Benedict.

"Labyrinths allow us to communicate with the world beyond," Rebecca said. "Since my first labyrinth walk I had dreamed of experiencing a labyrinth at the Louisville Seminary. Then in June 2002 a Chartres labyrinth was cut into the grass on campus. I was not able to walk it until August 3rd, the day of the memorial service for my late husband. As I entered the labyrinth and made three turns, a butterfly landed on my shoulder." Rebecca closed her eyes and smiled as if recalling her memory. Then she continued. "The lovely creature stayed about thirty minutes, fluttering a few feet away, then returning to rest on the same shoulder, the other shoulder and then on top of my head. For me, the butterfly was surely a renewed affirmation of resurrection and God's presence and grace."

"Very meaningful. No coincidence, I am sure," I said and nodded.

The sky turned indigo, inviting the night. My body was tired and exhausted. "It's time for me to go to bed. Thank you for letting me stay here. Have a good night, Rebecca." I got up, took a quick shower and soon after fell into a dreamless sleep.

4

The next morning a cool breeze, saturated with the scent of moist earth, awakened me. Rebecca had opened the porch door. Wild clouds stormed above. After a quick breakfast I put on my rain gear and rode to La Grange, 25 miles northeast of Louisville. Navigating the Suzuki on slippery wet roads congested with morning traffic required focus and concentration. My visor was cracked open, just to let enough air in so that it wouldn't fog up. I left the city behind and relaxed. Finally the sky cleared and the rain ceased. La Grange is a small town amidst green hills. I followed a country road along dairy farms. The white buildings of the Luther Luckett Correctional Complex looked out of place. I arrived at the front gate and the guard asked for identification.

"I am here to see Dr. Marc Wessels, the prison chaplain."

He looked on his list, nodded and waved me through.

The parking lot was filled with cars, but I found a free space close to the main entrance. Before entering I turned around, looked over the open green fields and saw cows grazing leisurely unaware of the troubles of the world.

I was asked to sign in and another guard took my ID and camera. This was my first visit to a prison and I was not familiar with the procedure. As I stepped through the metal detector, I saw Marc coming toward me, his arms open and a big inviting smile on his face. We had met during the labyrinth facilitator training. I liked Marc immediately; he stood out with his great sense of humor and unbound cheerfulness.

He welcomed me with a big hug. Marc was a man of strength - tall, with a black beard, short hair and friendly brown eyes. He wore dress pants and a multi-colored Hawaiian shirt.

Marc walked ahead of me and I followed him outside through a second secured gate. White walls fenced us in. We arrived at a modest brick building. Marc unlocked the door and we stepped into the entry room, which was lined with glass walls. I looked into three offices. The atmosphere was sterile and cold; the grey linoleum squeaked underneath our shoes. Marc unlocked another door. "Welcome to our chapel," he said. We entered the sacred space. A 7-circuit canvas labyrinth in a warm purple was laid out on the floor and almost filled the entire room.

I instantly felt at ease. The cathedral ceiling was made of light-colored pine wood and created a warm atmosphere. The high windows revealed barbed-wire fences and a cloudless sky. A fan buzzed in a pleasing monotonous rhythm. Colorful paintings hanging at eye height underneath the windows surrounded us. I took a closer look. Marc stood next to me.

"These are the Stations of the Cross," he said. "The drawings were created by the inmates. We offer art as a tool for rehabilitation. It allows these men, who may have known nothing but failure, to succeed at something."

The drawings were about 27 inches wide and 20 inches high. The inmates had depicted the different scenes in colored pencil, pencil, and watercolor. The picture of the crucifixion touched me deeply. The skilled artist revealed in precise detail and perfect anatomical proportions the death on the cross. Rich primary colors brought to life the suffering and agony. A dark sky loomed in the background.

"Wow, such incredible artistic talent," I said and then asked, "So, was there a lot of resistance to bringing the labyrinth into the prison?"

"Of course, the warden was very skeptical. He thought labyrinths were too new age," Marc laughed and then shook his head. "How can a labyrinth be new age? Our cars, computers and kitchen appliances are new age, but the Chartres labyrinth is 800 years old," he said.

"So what did you do to change his mind?"

"I invited two fellow labyrinth facilitators, who are Catholic, to organize an event with me in the gymnasium. They brought a canvas labyrinth and we had 78 inmates join for the first walk. It was incredible to see a secular space transformed into a sacred space. The warden was very impressed. We did two more events, and then he gave the green light to purchase a canvas labyrinth for our chapel and start the Labyrinth Program here."

Through the glass doors I saw the inmates, wearing khaki uniforms and tennis shoes, streaming into the entry room. Four younger men appeared to be in their early twenties, the older men in their forties and fifties.

"You will have everyone in this group," Marc explained. "There are murderers with life sentences, and sex-offenders, and the young men wearing the orange vests are imprisoned for drug-related charges. They got involved with burglary to pay for their drug habits or operated meth labs. Most of the men grew up without fathers; many never even knew their fathers. Sadly most men here did not get a lot of education."

We walked back to the entry room and Marc introduced me to the 14 men. I looked into their eyes; some did not return my gaze and looked down to the floor instead.

"Let's take off our shoes," Marc said.

We followed his instruction and then entered the chapel. I invited everyone to gather within the perimeters of the labyrinth. We stood in a circle and I asked the men to close their eyes. Then I guided the meditation with a soothing voice. I asked the men to visualize a ball of divine light above their heads and then bring this light through their breathing into their bodies and souls. As they exhaled, I suggested releasing everything that did not resonate with the benevolent light. I concluded the meditation by saying, "Imagine your whole being is filled with light; you are surrounded by light and you are the light. You are whole, balanced and complete, safe and secure, and all there is and all you experience now is radiant health, infinite joy, infinite love and infinite light on all levels."

I looked around in the circle. The men listened attentively to every word I said. Then I asked them to open their eyes again. No one avoided eye contact. "You may see your journey into the labyrinth as a meditative journey to unity. In our regular everyday consciousness, we perceive our world as a world of polarity. Opposites create one another. There is good and bad, right and wrong, day and night, sun and moon, male and female, and so forth. There is constant judgment and friction. The more we live in judgment, the more stress and unrest we experience and the harder it is to live a good life. The center of the labyrinth invites you to experience unity and non-judgment. Everything just is and has a right to exist."

I paused and looked at Marc. He gave me an encouraging smile.

"Do you all have issues you would like to release from your lives?"

The men nodded.

"Let's begin the journey. Who would like to be first?"

A young man wearing an orange vest stepped forward. I placed my hand on his shoulder, looked into his eyes, nodded and sent him off onto his journey. One by one the other men stepped forward. I touched everyone's shoulder, hoping it would make them feel more comfortable, and it also allowed me to tune into their energy fields.

Marc and I entered last. In a slow procession we moved through the twists and turns of the labyrinth. I felt the overwhelming weight of the men's burdens. The field of the labyrinth was heavy, as if covered by a dark cloud. I focused on breathing in the light.

For me, the labyrinth is a connecting device and it allows me to tune into people's energies, thoughts or even aches and pains. I had first learned about this phenomenon from a fellow labyrinth enthusiast. The first time she walked the labyrinth at the Chartres Cathedral in France, she had experienced severe hip pain. Every step she took became a burden, filled with agony. She was baffled by her experience. She reached the center and felt kinship with another woman her age, also in her fifties. She had never seen her before. They hugged and my friend continued her journey, suffering with pain. As mysteriously as she was overcome by the pain, it disappeared as soon as she exited the labyrinth. After the journey the group shared their insights. The woman whom my friend had hugged was very emotional and had tears in her eyes. She said, "I am disabled by severe hip problems. My entire adult life I have lived in pain. It is very difficult for me to walk. I was hesitant to join the labyrinth walk, but I was told I could take breaks and sit down if I needed. I am astonished because I did not need a chair to sit down or take a break. For the first time in my life, I have walked pain free. Every step was easy. It's a miracle. I can't wait to walk the labyrinth again."

My friend welled-up. She knew that the labyrinth had allowed her to take on the woman's pain, literally stepping into her shoes. She felt compassion for the woman's life journey and grateful for the opportunity to ease the pain.

I watched the men. They proceeded slowly and sincerely. I noticed a shift in energies; the field became lighter, as if a fresh breeze had swept through the room. My body responded in a positive way. My spine straightened, my chest opened and I began to breathe easily. To me, it felt that the more burdens the men released, the more light entered their fields of consciousness, uplifting all of us. I had witnessed this shift in energy during every labyrinth event I had facilitated and was happy to perceive an even greater intensity of release in this challenging environment. Finally, we all completed our journey and gathered within the labyrinth for a closing meditation.

"Do you all feel comfortable holding hands?" I asked.

"Yes," the men answered unanimously.

"So please join hands and let's form a circle of love. Please close your eyes and breathe in the divine light, feel it grow, expand and intensify with every breath you take." I guided the meditation with closed eyes and was amazed by what I saw in my mind's eye. "Now, look into your heart and affirm everything good that is there. Feel the light, the goodness and divine love entering your heart. As the light grows within your heart, you will be able to embrace your own divine qualities, your love, your beauty, your peace, your goodness and your divine essence." I saw dancing sparks of light filling the entire circle. "Now please open your eyes. Feel your connection to the Divine, and as you look at every person in our circle of love, see everyone else's divinity and goodness. Look at everyone with gratitude."

An incredible sense of peace filled the chapel; I felt something deep had moved within each man's consciousness. We opened our eyes and the young man who had entered the labyrinth first spoke out, "I never felt that I deserved anything good to happen to me. Now I do. I am very peaceful." The other men shared similar experiences.

Marc left for a brief moment. Everyone looked at him expectantly as he returned.

"We all would like to thank you for being here." Marc handed me a certificate of appreciation from the prison signed by him. One of the older men stepped forward and placed a cross into my hand. It was the size of my palm, crafted from copper wire and decorated with red strings. "It is handmade." He smiled.

"Thank you so much. The cross fits perfectly into the pocket of my motorcycle jacket," I said.

I shook hands with every inmate and thanked them for the gift, and they expressed their good-luck wishes for my journey.

"I hope to see you one day under better circumstances," said an older man, who in the beginning didn't dare to look into my eyes.

"It's a promise," I responded, and his face lit up.

The chapel emptied, Marc locked the door, and we went back to the main entrance where I picked up my ID and camera. We walked over to my bike. Marc gave me a big hug and we said goodbye. Then it was time for me to go and ride on.

I took the highway back into Louisville and headed for my next destination. The sun stood high. A few puffy clouds journeyed along the horizon. I reflected upon my experience and thought that in motorcycling, the most essential safety rule for group riding is that the weakest driver rides upfront. The group can go only as fast as its weakest member. This key element keeps the entire group safe.

In my eyes, Marc's pioneering rehabilitation work was an important part of the solution to an escalating problem. The United States' prison population is the highest in the world, having more people behind bars than any other nation. Coming from Germany, I had taken it for granted that a country would take care of the education and the welfare of all people. I had assumed that Americans also believe that society as a whole can be only as strong as its weakest link.

5

Sullivan University is located right off I-264. I turned into the university parking lot, left the bike in the shade underneath trees, and entered the reception office. As I opened the glass doors, the cool air-conditioned breeze streamed into my face. 'This feels good,' I thought and then told the secretary my name. She dialed Renee Rust Yarmuth, the wellness director. Renee and I met during our labyrinth facilitator training. She had started a labyrinth project on campus. When she first told me about her work, she emphasized that the labyrinth was located on land that had been worked by slaves.

Renee skipped down the steps. She was an energetic woman in her fifties. Short waves of black hair framed her gentle face. She was dressed in a casual business outfit, black pants and a blouse. Her movements were quick and dynamic, her voice soft. An aura of calmness surrounded her, a result of her 27 years in the quiet contemplative life of a Benedictine nun. She had left the order to take care of an ailing family member and then had realized that she wanted to share her life with someone.

"I'll show you the labyrinth. I don't have time to walk it with you, but meet me afterward and then we can chat," she said.

We walked on an unpaved road past the Farmington Historic Home, a historic Kentucky plantation home. Emerald green shutters framed the large windows of the expansive, elegant, red brick house. Tall trees provided cool shadows on this hot summer day. We walked past the historic blacksmith shop, a one-story brick building with white barn doors, and stepped out of the shade into the sweltering sun. Renee pointed to a field of wild, untamed grass. "Here it is," she said.

"Where?" I didn't see the labyrinth.

"Right here," Renee smiled. "Follow me."

A mowed pathway led through the tall and defiant grass. Then finally, I saw a pattern emerging. Renee explained that we stood at the entrance of a 100-foot Chartres replica.

A solid wall of evergreens blocked the view to the interstate, which bordered the property. The dominating sound of passing cars pierced my consciousness and felt too disturbing for a contemplative journey.

"I see the noise as the mantra of our modern world. I have become used to it and often find it soothing," Renee said. "I recommend walking the labyrinth with peace and liberty in mind, to transform the memory of suffering, which is stored in the earth. Have a good walk; I'll see you later." She waved a quick goodbye and left.

I approached the rugged labyrinth and took off my boots. The rough grass poked the bare soles of my feet, which prickled with every step. Still, I preferred to walk barefoot so that I could feel the earth. I tried to focus my attention on the suffering of the men and women who had labored this land. I imagined their faces and destinies and received the fleeting image of a male slave from an old newspaper ad that I had seen, in which a $100 reward had been offered for his capture. 'My pain is miniscule, even meaningless,' I thought. I knew nothing about suffering. My thoughts went on and on sucking me deeper into a dark abyss. The suffocating heat squeezed sweat out of every pore. I brushed away flies that buzzed all around. The cries of chirping crickets, louder than the traffic, overpowered everything. I felt on edge and in the labyrinth's center I found neither serenity nor relief. With every step I tried to walk away from the grief and sorrow only to fall further into a dark space. I wished for it to stop. Then an unsettling sense of void finally overcame me as I exited the labyrinth.

My gaze wandered to the wall of evergreens. The highway noise sliced into me, and my inner eye perceived nothing, no vision and no image. I had been sucked empty.

Exhausted, I walked back to Sullivan University to see Renee. We sat at a table in the cafeteria and drank cold iced tea.

"Wow, that was a really difficult labyrinth walk," I said. "If this experience is a reflection of my inner state of being, I must be a total mess. I hope I only picked up on the energy of the land. Then, still, some serious shifting and healing needs to happen."

"The land is burdened, there is no doubt," Renee nodded. "But you know, Dorit, the labyrinth does not always have to be a pleasant experience. Do you remember the candlelight walk during our facilitator training?"

"Yes, of course." I did remember the candlelight labyrinth walk. To me it was the highlight of our one-week training. A star-filled night sky had opened to infinity above the green lawns of the Presbyterian seminary. Seventy-five participants gathered to enter the labyrinth. Majestic trees surrounded the 66-foot grass labyrinth. Hundreds of candles had illuminated the night. They lit the winding path of the labyrinth.

"It sounds very romantic to walk at night with hundreds of candles," Renee continued. "But it was dark, and I was very anxious about losing my way. I followed a woman wearing white pants. I was so glad because the color was bright and I could follow her without getting lost. But suddenly she stepped off her path and walked away from the labyrinth. I was worried and fearful, and it was difficult to find my own path. But then, of course, there is a deeper meaning. The labyrinth is always a metaphor for life."

"Interesting," I said. "I saw the woman in the white pants, too. I was intrigued by her and watched her for a while. I had a completely different experience; to me it was a special night." I recalled that Dr. Lauren Artress, a tall woman with short silver hair and sparkling wise eyes, stood at the labyrinth's entrance. She paced us and shared her wisdom as we embarked on our journey.

I went on to tell Renee that my turn had come after 50 fellow seekers already entered the labyrinth. I felt mesmerized by their unison of rhythm, as if a higher force invisibly directed a melodic dance of silence and peace. It was the first time I had walked a labyrinth with that many people. When I began my journey, Dr. Lauren Artress smiled and said, "A silent experience breaks barriers."

I followed the path, meandered slowly toward the center, toward unity and enlightenment. A harpist played soft tunes. I heard celestial music and the hymns of angels and dove deeper into the meditative experience.

Even though we all followed our own path at our own pace, we were connected as one human family. An invisible force had brought us together.

One woman cried out, tears streamed down her face. Simultaneously, a woman dressed in white pants stepped out of the labyrinth. She had short brown hair, and I estimated her age to be early sixties. First she walked away turning her back, but after a while she returned and sat in the grass. She watched. Her face expressed anger and rebellion.

Her action had seemed so unusual that at first I focused on her, but then my attention was drawn back to the many people with whom I had crossed paths. Participants stopped and hugged each other.

Others stepped aside in silence, stared down, and avoided eye contact. A man stomped his feet in the grass; he looked upset. In the labyrinth there was no place to hide. Our true and most vulnerable selves emerged.

I felt familiar with the vast variety of emotions that I saw within my fellow seekers. Yes, I have lived through every single one of them. I have loved and hated, and felt anger, fear, despair and frustration. I have had days when I was exuberant with joy and a few times when I couldn't even see the beacon of light that brings optimism and the will to live. I have been hurt and I have hurt others, mostly the ones I love. I knew too well the painful heartache of a loved one's betrayal. I have been excluded and separated, but have also experienced the all encompassing bliss of belonging and community. Every one of my life lessons has made me who I am today.

I reached the center and said a wholehearted "Yes." Peace settled into my soul like an old friend, extinguishing the memories of drama and struggle. I journeyed back to the labyrinth's entrance.

The older man who had been upset earlier walked next to me. He passed the woman sitting in the grass, stopped, reached out to her, helped her up and hand in hand they continued to walk together. Later I learned they were husband and wife.

"In the labyrinth, we meet only ourselves," Renee concluded. "We see only what we need to learn at the moment. It's a beautiful tool for spiritual transformation." She stood up. "Thank you for stopping by. I have to get back to work." We hugged each other, said goodbye, and then I rode on. The picture of the husband and wife stayed with me, his hand reaching out and then pulling her toward him. And I wondered why this day filled with labyrinth experiences relating to lack of freedom and imprisonment concluded with thoughts about marriage.

6

Wednesday morning, August 16. My journey continued on I-64 across the Ohio River into Indiana. Pleasant temperatures, an open azure sky, and gently floating white clouds allowed for a gorgeous day of riding. The scent of green cow pastures reminded me of my home in Germany. I enjoyed an excellent ride, cruising at the maximum allowed speed, when I recalled a dream from the night before. Immediately my great mood got even better. In my dream I saw children playing in a labyrinth. They ran, jumped and rejoiced. Their innocent laughter uplifted my soul. The children's exuberant playfulness and ease erased the heaviness and weight I carried from the demanding labyrinth walk of the previous day.

Sixty carefree miles later, I pulled off the highway into Ferdinand, a charming small town with German roots. I let the bike roll to a fuel station and parked at the pump next to two BMW motorcycles, a black GS 1150 and a yellow GS 1200. Both had Pennsylvania license plates. I had considered getting a bigger bike for this road trip and tested the GS 1150, a superb machine. But I decided that my comfortable Suzuki Bandit 600 had sufficient power to cross the country.

As I filled my tank with premium fuel, a couple in their forties, fully geared in protective leathers, walked over from the shop.

"Hello," the woman said. Like me, she had her long hair pulled back into a ponytail.

"Where are you heading?"

29

"Out West, to California."

"My husband and I are on our way from Philadelphia to visit friends in Denver. Are you traveling by yourself?"

"Yes, I am on a road trip to walk labyrinths."

"Labyrinths, what's that?" the husband asked.

"It is a walking meditation. Labyrinths are round structures found in every culture around the globe, dating back thousands of years." I showed them the labyrinth picture on my tank bag.

"I have seen this pattern before," the woman said and then asked, "You can meditate with it?"

"Yes, it's a one-way path that leads you to the center. It helps to focus your mind."

"So it's like a maze?" the husband asked.

"No. In a maze you make choices. A maze is designed to confuse, and it activates your rational and conscious thinking. In a labyrinth, you follow a one-way path, and there are no choices. You can let go of your reasoning and thinking and enter altered and higher states of consciousness."

"Interesting. So you are the mellow biker," he said.

"Maybe. I don't know," I laughed.

"Well, it is nice to meet you. Good luck on your journey," the wife said.

We put on our helmets and drove off waving our goodbyes. I followed the directions to the next labyrinth. I came to a standstill at a turn and checked the map on my tank bag. The picture next to it drew my attention. It was a photograph of one of my oil paintings. Six months before, I had recorded my third meditation CD, which was also my first dual purpose CD. A listener can meditate in a sitting or lying position or while walking a labyrinth. I enjoyed designing the CD cover, on which I painted an indigo labyrinth on an abstract light blue background. The colors were brought to life by accentuating strokes of bright yellow and red. One of my clients, intrigued by the art, had commissioned a labyrinth painting for her meditation room. I liked the idea of painting labyrinths and an entire series followed. The gallery at the Westminster Presbyterian Church displayed my new creations. Six of the nine colorful labyrinth paintings sold and the profits paid for my road trip. To me, it felt as if the spiritual force, from which the labyrinths originated, took care of me. Everything had fallen into place.

I also learned one memorable and haunting lesson about the sacred power of the labyrinth. In preparation for the labyrinth series I bought ten empty canvases. I lined them up along the walls in my studio. They stared at me with their bright white emptiness. I sat down in the middle of the room and meditated. I loved the excited anticipation of not yet knowing what would reveal itself to me on these canvases.

For me, inspired art makes the invisible worlds visible and enables the viewer to enter heightened states of awareness. My responsibility as an artist is to be clear-minded and connected to the source when I paint.

Layer by layer, the abstract background began to breathe. Multiple coats of oil colors created depth. Blue and red were the primary foundations. Several weeks later, I completed the backgrounds. The slow process of drawing the 11-circuit Chartres pattern on the canvases started. I was baffled to find that I needed frequent breaks when I worked on the labyrinth pattern. After only two hours I felt lightheaded, and my mind was spinning. In the past, I had amazing dreams of colors after long days spent in my studio. Now, I just closed my eyes and saw streams of colors, like rivers of inspiration, streaming in front of my inner eye. I went for a walk or a jog to ground myself and then returned to the canvas.

I completed the first four labyrinth patterns. In order for the color to dry, I placed them in the back of the studio. One of the paintings, a viridian green labyrinth on a sky blue background looked pale. It was quiet and introspective in comparison to the red, yellow and vibrant blue labyrinths. I grabbed the canvas, put it on the easel and with quick brushstrokes I added bright yellow and red on top of the labyrinth pattern. I was shocked to feel the labyrinth's energy field collapse. The gentle hum of the field, the light that cleared my mind and brought peace were gone. A void of nothingness screamed. A tunnel of blackness absorbed me. It felt as though my whole world had disintegrated in front of my eyes. I did not know that something like this was possible and was shaken by this unintended result. My own hand, which painted this beautiful labyrinth, destroyed it in one thoughtless, unreflective moment. I couldn't stand seeing the violated labyrinth, so I turned it toward the wall.

Immediately I called my Israeli friend, Batia, to come to my studio. She admired the paintings and smiled.

"Dorit, these are incredible, so powerful. I love them."

"Wait before you say anything. You have to see this one." I turned the one canvas that faced the wall. Batia's facial expression changed. Eyes wide open she stared at the painting; she was speechless.

"What do you think?" I asked.

"Oh my God, it looks like war." She inhaled deeply, as if gasping for air. "There is so much pain and violence. I can't look at it."

"You see what happened." I pointed out areas on the painting. "I added only a few brush strokes of colors on top of the labyrinth pattern, and they destroyed the entire field."

Batia turned her head away. "Wow, I can't look at it. It's too raw."

I put the canvas back in its place, facing the wall.

"Thank you for coming over. You are very intuitive, and I needed to be sure that I am not totally out of my mind. You feel exactly what I feel."

Batia was the only confidante to see the painting. After she left, I took the canvas off the wooden frame, cut it carefully with scissors into small pieces and disposed of it. In spite of this, I was unable to erase its memory, still a haunting reminder of the sacrilege I had committed.

This experience taught me a lesson about the mystery of the labyrinth. We don't know who created them. All information is lost in time. But the labyrinth asks us to respect its sacredness and treat it with reverence. Most important, we are not to alter its original blueprint. It is perfect, the way it is.

I continued to the right and drove up a hill. I marveled at the massive red brick buildings of the Monastery Immaculate Conception on top of a hill, overlooking the town of Ferdinand and the rolling countryside. I continued past the monastery gift shop called 'For Heaven's Sake' to the grass labyrinth, named the Hildegard of Bingen labyrinth, in honor of the medieval mystic. A wave of children's laughter traveled toward me. The labyrinth, surrounded by acres of green lawns and old trees, spread out its perfect beauty. A dozen children ran along the labyrinth's winding path, dashing forward, competing with each other to reach the center. Surprised, I realized that I had seen this precise image in my dream last night. A short while later the children, whom I estimated to be between eight and twelve years old, strolled off.

I centered myself at the labyrinth's entrance, stepped forward and followed the one-way path. My mind took me back in time to the moment when Batia and I had first met. The year was 1999 and I was new to Pittsburgh. While phoning friends in Israel I had noticed that Hebrew words would escape my vocabulary. I needed to practice so as not to lose the language. In my daily meditations, I had included a request to find an Israeli friend with whom I could enjoy Hebrew conversations.

A few weeks later, I accepted an invitation and went to my first women's networking event at a hospital. We mingled, talking about our professions, while waiters served hors d'oeuvres and wine. The majority of women were dressed in elegant business outfits and wore perfect make-up and high heels. Out of place, I wore black pants, my favorite rainbow-colored knitted sweater, comfortable walking shoes, and no make-up. Concluding that this was not my kind of event, I finished drinking a glass of wine, packed up the information material and got ready to leave. Precisely at that moment two women approached me. One was German and thought I was, too, because of my family name; the other woman was Israeli.

"Dorit, you are not leaving yet, I have been looking for you all over. I saw your flyers. I am Batia," she said in Hebrew. Her features indicated a Polish heritage, her face round and gentle, her eyes an inquiring bright blue.

"Where are you from?" she asked.

"Germany."

"Germany? I would have thought you are Israeli. Your name is Israeli."

"I lived and studied in Israel."

"Interesting. Which school did you go to?"

"Mahut in Tel Aviv. I studied with Gilad Shadmon."

"Are you serious?" Batia laughed. "I know Gilad very well. His first wife is my best childhood friend."

We ordered more wine and engaged in a lively conversation. A few days later, I visited Batia's home in Pittsburgh for the first time. She showed me her wedding pictures and I recognized Gilad among the guests. Batia and I became good friends, and we enjoyed speaking Hebrew, even though she was fluent in German. In 1989, the year I moved to Israel, she moved to Germany.

I marveled at the interconnectedness of all events, enjoyed my labyrinth walk and perceived a sense of all-expansive happiness, as if the field were still charged with the children's presence. Then I rode on.

7

My journey continued West on I-64. An hour later, I turned off the highway to follow the directions to historic New Harmony, Indiana. I rode on a solitary winding road, surrounded by endless fields of tall standing corn.

New Harmony was founded in 1814 by the Harmony Society, a group of Separatists from the German Lutheran Church. In 1825 Robert Owen, a Welsh-born industrialist and social philosopher, bought the Indiana town and the surrounding lands for his communitarian experiment. A few years later, the community dissolved due to constant quarrels.

I entered the little town and passed the historic storefronts. Picturesque and artfully designed gables towered above souvenir shops, antique stores and restaurants. I turned onto a side street, passed log houses and then parked my bike next to the Sacred Meditation Garden, ready for the second labyrinth walk of the day. The labyrinth was an 11-circuit Chartres replica. The polished black granite reflected the sun, and I anticipated a gorgeous walk on the smooth and warm surface. Still energized from my earlier walk, I had no particular subject in mind to meditate upon, so I considered dedicating this walk to gratitude and thankfulness.

I centered myself at the labyrinth's entrance. A canopy of trees provided a pleasant shadow on this hot and humid afternoon. The cool scent of trickling fountain water peacefully engulfed the magnificent meditation garden, which was designed according to the dimensions of the nave in the Chartres Cathedral. I took a step forward into the labyrinth and was startled by a shocking discovery. The labyrinth pushed me back, not allowing me to enter. I hit an invisible wall. I stumbled and then stepped back, shocked by what had happened. I took a few deep breaths and then reached out with both hands. I felt resistance and a dense stream of energy trembled against my palms, pushing me away. Carefully, I moved my left foot forward, but the labyrinth was sealed. I closed my eyes to check if I would receive more information about this unknown phenomenon. But my mind's eye went blank.

Baffled, I looked around. There was not another person there; only a few cows grazed in the open meadow across from me. I noticed a young red beech tree. We have one just like it in the garden on our family farm in Germany.

I was tempted to try entering the labyrinth one more time. Instead, I decided to take a few deep breaths and then bowed deeply. My fingertips touched the sun-warmed granite. I was on a journey of respect and surrender. There were bigger forces at work than my human mind could perceive. I had to trust that it was not time for me to walk this labyrinth.

Mystified, I drove off to the opposite end of town to see the famous hedge maze. Originally it had been created as a labyrinth. For the Harmonists, it represented the difficult path of life to reach true harmony and perfection. Reconstructed in 1939, the labyrinth had been transformed into a maze – with choices of paths to take.[1] Openings in the hedges allowed me to walk directly to the center, to a small round one-room building. The rooftop spire reached straight to the sky. During the time of the Harmonists a 'blind door' opened to the elegant and peaceful interior; this day the room appeared to be barren and empty. I let my fingers run along the irregular natural stone wall as I circled the building. I didn't stay.

Even though I found myself in a paradise of hedges and tall green trees, I felt no connection or depth. I was overcome by the sudden urgency to move on. Quickly I returned to my bike and unfolded the map. I was 150 miles east of St. Louis, Missouri, and realized that in a couple of hours I would hit rush hour traffic. While figuring the best route around the city, I saw a contractor's white pickup truck pull up next to me.

"Need any help?" the driver asked. He was a man in his fifties with short spiky hair and a friendly smile.

"Yes."

He got out of his truck and examined the map. "Best way for you to go at this time of day is 255 to 270 and then you get onto 44." His finger traced the itinerary on my map.

"Thank you so much," I said.

"Sure thing. Have a good trip." He waved, got back into his truck and drove off.

I pulled out shortly afterward and followed the winding country road. Then I got on the highway and opened the throttle. A couple of hours later I reached St. Louis. The Gateway Arch, a shining monument called the gateway to the west, rose to over 600 feet tall. I crossed the Mississippi River on the Jefferson Barracks Bridge as rush hour traffic slowed me down to twenty miles per hour. I merged onto I-44, and the flow of vehicles heading to the suburbs halted to a near standstill. I was sweaty, overheated and tired. I opened my jacket halfway for some air. Relieved, I reached my exit and continued onto the scenic country road 100. The setting sun turned the sky into a spectacle of orange and purple while I drove through charming little towns in the Missouri River Valley. Colorful signs invited travelers to visit the numerous wineries. I cruised along farms. Lazy cows leisurely grazed on their pastures.

Finally I reached my destination, the German community of Hermann, nestled along the banks of the river, in the heart of the Missouri wine country. While researching my itinerary I had been attracted to the promise of old world hospitality and the typical German names for a bed and breakfast like Birk, Wohlt and Neufeld, located on Goethestreet, Schillerstreet or Weinstreet.

I had fantasized about finding a sweet little town with flair and character resembling my hometown, Rees, in Germany. Founded in 1228, Rees is the oldest city in the Lower Rhine Valley. An extensive promenade adjacent to the medieval city wall invites a stroll along the River Rhine. Contemporary sculptures by young artists are on display year-round, and detailed bronze sculptures illuminate the city's rich history. On any given summer day, pedestrians and bicyclists can enjoy the relaxed atmosphere on the promenade. They stop in the cafés or beer gardens for refreshments or a meal, while watching the ships on the river go by. People are friendly, they smile often and say 'Hello' even to complete strangers, and it is easy to engage in conversations.

Hermann was deserted of all souls; not a single person was out on the streets. Slowly I drove past the one open restaurant, and a dozen empty tables stared at me. There was no promenade next to the river, only an asphalt parking lot. It was mid-week and I concluded that this town awakened only on the weekends. Disappointed, I stopped and pulled out my maps.

I was traveling by myself, and the thought of a solitary dinner made me quiver. I wanted people around, music, noise, and conversations at the neighboring table that I could listen in to. My long day of motorcycle riding had been quiet and introspective. I needed life around me.

I rode on, my heart filled with longing for my hometown or something familiar, yet fleeting, something I couldn't grasp. Then, all of a sudden, my mind wrapped itself around the day of my dad's funeral eight years ago and focused entirely on one instance. My father had died unexpectedly after an emergency surgery on his colon, only two weeks after I had arrived in the United States. I had seen him last at my farewell party in Düsseldorf. Distressed, I traveled back to Germany. After the funeral my dad's lifelong friend Gerhard approached me.

"You know, Dorit," he said as he placed his hand on my shoulder, "your dad rode a motorcycle when he was young."

I shook my head and said, "No way."

"Yes, he did. He drove a red BMW motorcycle. He had an awful crash and never touched it again."

I was speechless and recalled the many times my dad had hammered into my mind that girls don't ride motorbikes. It was an ongoing battle. During my teenage years I had vivid dreams in which I rode at exhilarating speeds on a motorcycle, the landscape flying by. When I leaned into the wind and opened the throttle, joy swept my entire being. All boundaries vanished. I felt more alive than ever. Upon awakening, I had been euphoric and invigorated, and I knew one day I would ride a bike of my own.

But my dad was strict, and he demanded that I never ride a bike, never study art or never dare to follow my lofty dreams. He said that the reality is different than what I imagined. He pointed out that life is a struggle, and I would learn that soon enough.

I hated his beliefs but also attributed his thinking to his narrow perception of the role of a woman and how good girls were supposed to behave. I had never wondered if there was a deeper underlying cause for his aversion of motorcycles. Later, after I had moved to Israel and bought my first bike, a red Czechoslovakian Jawa 350, my father acted as if I had committed the most horrendous crime. When I mentioned the bike, he abruptly ended the conversation. So I never talked about it again.

I looked into Gerhard's steel blue eyes and asked, "What happened?"

"He flew out of a curve, was going too fast. He crashed into a field and barely missed a big tree that would have killed him for sure. He walked away with bruises, no serious injuries. But that shook him up pretty well. He was lucky to survive."

We looked silently into each others eyes. It felt as if time stood still, then Gerhard said, "Dorit, that all happened long before you were born."

I wondered if my father had felt the same unbound joy of being out in the elements, his face in the wind. I wondered that maybe decades ago he had loved to ride his red BMW just as much as I loved to ride my machine.

I pressed on to I-70, and at nightfall I arrived in the college town of Columbia. I took the exit with the greatest number of signs advertising hotels and immediately drove by a variety of restaurants. Applebee's was the only one familiar. Exhausted from riding 455 miles in one day, I pulled into the parking lot. I had no energy left for surprises or disappointments. I sat next to a window where I could see my fully packed bike. Young people at the tables next to me chattered and laughed, while I indulged in a hearty meal of steak, potatoes, and steamed vegetables and a big glass of beer. After dinner I drove to the closest hotel, a modern Wingate, checked in, unloaded the bike, called Frank, took a hot shower, got underneath soft bed sheets and fell asleep immediately.

In the middle of the night, I jolted back into consciousness. I opened my eyes to a semi-dark room, at first not realizing where I was. In my dream, I was back at the grass labyrinth at Sullivan University, which I had walked in Louisville. In my hotel room I still felt profoundly connected to the labyrinth. I had walked the sacred path to honor the enslaved men and women who had labored the land. In my dream, I saw my painful and tiring journey from a heightened perspective and watched myself as I exited the labyrinth. I saw my disappointed facial expression, sweat streamed across my forehead, and I noticed the slow heavy movements of my limbs. I was fully absorbed and disempowered by embracing the anguish of the men and women who had suffered on this land. My energy field had shrunk to a small flickering light, barely visible. I had forgotten that true healing comes only by entering the source of all good, the all-embracing light beyond good and evil, instead of connecting to the ache and agony.

My walk had not been in vain, though. The moment I left the labyrinth something happened to its field. From the observer position in my dream, I saw it vividly. I also heard a sound, like the clinking of glass or very loud high-pitched chimes. It was a sound that could rip things apart and it intensified. The earth underneath the labyrinth trembled, the tall grass shook back and forth rapidly. The ground burst open and the labyrinth birthed shimmering red and clear crystals. Thousands of crystals moved upwards, lifted by an unseen force. I understood they represented sweat, tears and blood. The clinking became louder while the shiny crystals rose in a fast swirling vortex upward. The vast open sky danced with bright sunrays of rainbow colors, emanating from the crystals. Eventually, it all stopped, the earth was free and a bright tower of light extended from the labyrinth all the way up to the heavens.

I switched on the bedside table lamp, penned a few notes in my journal, thought to myself that this was a really wild dream and went back to sleep.

8

The fourth day of my journey, I got up late, at 9:00 a.m. I had scheduled an appointment at 1:00 p.m. in Sibley, Missouri, and estimated the drive to be an hour and a half. At 11:30 a.m., my bike was fully packed and ready to go. I carefully balanced it as I pushed it off the center stand. The engine started with its perfect roar, inviting a great day of riding. I continued on I-70 heading west. Well rested, happy and free, I hummed joyfully in my helmet. The sky was an endless light aqua, the temperature was warm, and I was living my dream.

An hour later I took the Blue Springs exit and followed a country road, riding over rolling hills along farms and meadows with grazing cows and horses. A sudden shift occurred in the way I felt in my body. A distinctive sense of lightness had logged in to my nervous system. I was thoroughly grounded in my body, operating my motorcycle. I pressed the rear brakes gently as I prepared to turn onto a one-lane road. Then I opened the throttle and accelerated. At the same time, a tingling sensation touched me all over; I was immersed in a vibration of light that communicated with me. Astonished, I looked around and scanned the view. My gaze was locked in to the distance on a grove of trees. I could not take my eyes away, or turn my head or focus on anything else. Instinctively I knew that this was the location of the labyrinth.

The twisty road brought me closer. I passed tall hedges and pulled into the driveway in front of a white farmhouse. I did not see the labyrinth, but I felt it. Three barking dogs stormed toward me. I stopped the engine and the dogs calmed down. They wagged their tails, begging to be petted. A charismatic blond woman in her early fifties greeted me with a big smile. She was slender, dressed in black leggings, a T-shirt and flip flops.

"Hello, I am Toby," she said. Toby Evans is an artist, musician, spiritual counselor and a founding member of The Labyrinth Society, an international organization inspiring possibilities and creating connections through the labyrinth. I had posted a request for information about outdoor labyrinths on the Labyrinth Facilitator Network. Toby was the first to respond.

"Let's go to the studio; we can sit down and chat, and then I'll show you the labyrinth."

We entered a separate building that opened into one big space. The walls were decorated with impressive works of art. Toby created six-foot high mandalas, composed of natural and scavenged materials like twigs, feathers, bones, animal skulls, clay fiber, mirror pieces and metal. One piece titled *Cyclic Whole* showed four separate organic areas swirling into one circular mirror area.

Toby brought two glasses of water, and we sat on a comfortable sofa. She showed me her book, *Keeper of the Circles, Answering the Call to Wholeness*. The cover displayed a picture of one of her paintings, showing her dancing in her labyrinth. The horizon was covered with swirling flames. The unique perspective opened the view into the earth, revealing a dome of underground water. Toby danced in the four elements, earth, water, fire and air. The labyrinth circled through her body.

"I am so excited you are here. When I wrote this book I envisioned that there would be people like you. What you do is very important." She opened her book and said, "I would like for you to hear this. It is a chapter about the different tasks associated with the labyrinths." She read aloud with a mesmerizing soft voice, "And then there are the 'Field Connectors.' These individuals are inspired to physically travel from one site to the next. By doing so, the energy fields are connected through their own bodies. As modern day pilgrims, they bring the power of one earth pattern to the next, strengthening the circuit and uniting the grid. Their adventurous spirits record and report the details to fill out the bigger picture."

I smiled. Toby radiated open-minded creativity. I enjoyed her peaceful and confident presence and felt a deep bond of kinship, as if she were a good old friend whom I had known for many years.

"It is so appropriate that you travel by motorcycle; you are out in the elements, not confined in a car. Your energy field grows with every labyrinth you walk. Being outside enables you to hold the energy and integrate it into your own field."

"Yes, I know," I said, happy to meet a person with whom I could openly talk about spiritual phenomena that under any other circumstance I would keep only to myself. "So, tell me about your labyrinth," I said. "It is the biggest one in the United States, 166 feet. And it is very powerful. I tuned into its vibration when I was two miles away."

"Great. So you are sensitive to energies," Toby responded.

"Yes." I paused and then asked, "So, has this land always belonged to your family?"

"No, my husband and I were both teachers in the public school system in Iowa. I taught art and Bruce was a science teacher. In 1987 we moved to Kansas when he accepted a Science Resource position with the Kansas City School District. He picked a home in a nice suburban neighborhood, and I agreed to use the basement for my studio. We had already put money down and the papers were being processed. Then the federal government bought the house out from under us. Our realtor was in disbelief. This was unheard of. For me, it was a confirmation that it wasn't ours and there was a higher power in action." Toby smiled. "I began to look for properties in the outlying areas of Kansas City, anything that had outbuildings.

When I first saw this farm I wasn't impressed at all. The house was a wreck and needed a lot of fixing up. Bruce expressed a decisive 'No.' But our realtor said one sentence that stuck with me. She said that the soybean field behind the farm was currently leased out for extra income. But if we would buy the farm we could do with the field whatever we wanted. I began to see the field in my dreams. There was something about this place that wouldn't let me go. I was convinced that we belonged here. But how could I persuade my scientist husband who didn't believe in prophetic dreams or inner voices? I remembered his idea to have a prairie restoration project and suggested that he could seed the field with native grasses. And you know what he said?"

I shook my head.

"He said: 'Yeah and I could mow paths through it and bring school groups out to teach them about the prairie and the different ecosystems.'" Toby smiled, "Suddenly his resistance was gone. It was a magic moment, everything started falling into place and it all happened before I even knew about labyrinths."

"So when did you learn about labyrinths?" I asked.

"In 1994 two close friends told me about labyrinths. They had learned about a walking meditation at a dowsing conference and asked me to come to the next meeting. I was skeptical and unfamiliar with dowsing, which as my friends explained allows us to step beyond human limitations and obtain information from a higher level of consciousness. And I was not at all interested in finding my way through a frustrating maze. My friends assured me that a labyrinth and a maze are two different things. At the conference I met Kay Torrez. She had orchestrated building seven different labyrinths in the desert outside Gila Bend, Arizona, before her death in 2000. Four of the labyrinths represented the four elements, earth, water, air and fire. Kay called her desert labyrinth site The Labyrinth Pharmacy. She prescribed the combination of labyrinth patterns best suited for the individuals who came to walk them by dowsing what their energy field needed at the moment."

"A Labyrinth Pharmacy. Wow, that sounds very progressive," I said.

"Yes, and at the conference she researched the effect of finger-walking a labyrinth on the person's auric energy field and their chakra system," Toby continued to explain. "Chakra is a Sanskrit word for the energetic force centers of our spiritual bodies. She was doing this by dowsing with a pendulum, measuring each person's existing aura and then checking to see if the individual's chakras were open or closed. I followed this preliminary procedure and then sat down to a table of crayons, where I was given a paper with an outline of a 7-circuit labyrinth. I was instructed to color in the paths using the rainbow colors that correspond with the seven chakras. When I finished, Kay told me to trace the pattern with my finger and then to charge it by holding it against a photograph of one of her existing labyrinths called 'The Power Labyrinth.' She then measured my aura and rechecked my chakras. Kay recorded that all of my chakras, including the three that were closed prior to coloring, were open in the post measuring procedure. My aura expanded from an initial 4 feet in diameter to 179 feet. I knew that something was going on. I knew then that I was to build a labyrinth and the design would be a classical 7-circuit with a large central circle."

Toby stood up and grabbed two copper rods from a shelf. "Let's go outside. I would like to measure your energy field and then I'll show you the labyrinth."

"I have never seen these dowsing devices before. Can I take a look?" I asked.

"Sure. These are called L rods." Toby handed me the rods. I placed the short-ended handle in my hand and the foot-long end swung freely.

"Interesting. I have only used pendulums for dowsing, and in Germany, the Y rods are popular for finding water lines or negative energetic disturbances," I said.

Toby opened the door and her dogs, Daisy, a boxer, Sparky, a golden collie and coyote mix, and Butch, a pit bull, trotted next to us as we walked by a 12-foot medicine wheel which was laid out in base quartz crystal and sand.

"Stand right here," Toby instructed me. I stopped on an open patch of lawn and Toby placed the dowsing rods in front of her chest pointing away from her body. Then she took slow steps toward me and suddenly the rods swung out of control left and right and then crossed each other.

"This is the size of your energy field." She stepped toward me and counted her steps. "One, two, three, four, five; your field extends five feet beyond your physical body. That's pretty good."

"I don't have a reference point, so I'll take your word for it," I laughed.

"Dowsing shows the profound effect of the labyrinth. I'll measure your energy field after the walk, and then you will see the difference," she said.

We approached her labyrinth and the living ocean of six-foot tall prairie grass swayed with the wind. A mowed path opened into the field and I followed Toby. We stopped at a wooden fence post. Rainbow colored strings fluttered in the wind. A quartz crystal on top of the post pointed to the sky and an image showed the layout of the chakra labyrinth and a butterfly, the universal symbol for transformation.

"This is the labyrinth's entrance," she said.

We took a few steps farther to a second fence post, wrapped with red strings. A single wind chime played a rhythmic deep clink. An angel, sculpted in clay, had been placed at eye level. The detailed work of art showed the angel's soft face and blue eyes gazing into the distance. An emblem of the labyrinth pattern and encircling earthy roots decorated the red robe. Feathered wings, like blossoms of a rose, embraced the angel's shoulders.

"This is the root chakra angel," Toby said. "At the turns you will find reflection stations to inform you of the correlations between the path you are on and the chakras. They are a reminder for release and renewal. The sound of the chime corresponds to the specific chakra. I'll show you another one." Toby parted the wall of prairie grass with both arms, and we stepped through the opening into the turn of the solar plexus chakra. A yellow angel gazed at me with warm open eyes. A thumb-sized crystal was embedded underneath its chest, reflecting rays of sunlight. The labyrinth outlines were etched underneath. The angel's wings spread open into a spacious flowing motion. The chime played a higher pitch than the first one.

The dogs barked and jumped through the wall of tall grass, running mischievously along the path. We laughed and Toby clapped her hands, "Daisy, Sparky, Butch, come on, time to go." She parted the grass and we walked back to the entrance.

"I will leave you now. You will have total privacy during your labyrinth walk."

"Thank you, Toby," I answered.

She hesitated for a moment. "There is one more thing I would like to suggest. On special occasions, for example a full moon celebration, I walk the labyrinth naked. I would not say this to everybody, but you are open-minded and I trust you. If you walk the labyrinth naked you will feel a special connection to nature." She winked her eyes, called her dogs and walked off.

9

Left alone, I stood next to the fence post that marked the labyrinth's entrance. The air burst with scents of prairie grasses native to the area; Big Blue Stem, Indian grass and Switch grass. I took off my boots and socks and stretched my feet, then slid out of my leather pants and took off my T-shirt and bra. The wind tickled my bare skin. I let my underpants drop to the ground and last I took off the necklace I had received from Frank. After folding my clothes into a neat pile, I placed them on the grass next to the fence post.

Naked I embarked into the labyrinth. The soft warm carpet of mowed grass laid out the path in front of me. Tall grass engulfed me affectionately. I was comfortable and at ease. The sun stood high, sending rays of heat. Sweat trickled out of the pores of my skin.

My vision was focused on only my immediate area; I saw less than twenty feet ahead. As I proceeded, I recognized a sudden loss of orientation. The waving ocean of grass that had caressed my skin moments earlier transformed into towering walls fencing me in. I began gasping for air; baffled by the shift I could think only of a deep urge to flee. My legs were shaky. I ran forward, then halted, turned and spun around my own axis. I ran back, stopped and turned again. My hands clenched into fists. 'This is crazy,' I thought, 'What is happening to me?' I pushed myself to focus on breathing in the light and breathing out whatever force had overcome me. It didn't feel that it was my nakedness that overwhelmed me but rather the sudden loss of orientation and feeling fenced in, even imprisoned.

There was no escape. 'I do not know how long the journey ahead will be, but it will be long,' I thought. And I had just started. The effort of focused attention brought a release.

My legs stopped shaking and my strength returned to me. The only person I could meet during this solitary labyrinth walk was me; my emotions, my shadows, the hidden aspects of my personality. I felt raw and unprotected, as if my soul were laid out open in front of me. I had chosen this path, and my task was to walk it. 'Or had the path chosen me?' I wondered. I continued to breathe in the light, contemplating that if I shined the light into the shadow, the shadow would vanish. I had no choice but to surrender and meet myself, whoever that might be.

Light, fast steps took me farther into the labyrinth. I completed the second turn and I tried to exhale my need to be in control and to know where I was going. I had to trust the path, without understanding the bigger picture. My mind calmed down and my thoughts cleared, like a peaceful surface of a shimmering lake on a bright summer day.

An insight emerged. Life must be lived forward but only made sense by looking backward. Only in retrospect do the pieces of the puzzle connect, revealing an intelligently orchestrated evolution. Our journey through life is in a way like walking blindfolded.

Peacefully I arrived at the third turn. A chime's high-pitched sound resonated within my body and unplugged an opening underneath my ribcage. It felt as if my lungs had grown bigger and I had inhaled a greater volume of oxygen. A fresh breeze engulfed me, awakening me with a cool pleasant shiver.

Suddenly I heard a buzzing from above; the noise came closer and I lifted my head. A bright yellow vintage biplane flew over me. The pilot sat in an open cockpit. I couldn't believe my eyes and kept on walking, trying to not think about this peculiar occurrence. But it was impossible to ignore the biplane, as it flew a loop and then circled above the labyrinth. 'So much for total privacy,' I thought, wondering if the pilot had ever seen a labyrinth pattern, and a naked woman walking it. I was exposed and there was no way to escape or to not be seen. Thoughts flooded my consciousness.

'Everything that happens in the labyrinth is a metaphor.'

'There is a deeper meaning.'

'Look up and see. There is a lesson for you to be learned.'

'You are on the yellow path and it's a yellow biplane. Don't you see the connection?'

'The outside world is a reflection of the inside world.'

'The pilot navigating the biplane high in the sky is a reflection of your own higher self.'

'The pilot sees the bigger picture.'

'Rise above your limited vision and see where you are in relation to the entirety of things.'

I acknowledged every thought that entered my mind. Eventually I didn't care anymore that I was being seen naked. 'So what,' I said aloud to myself. There was nothing I could do about it anyhow.

I still had to walk my path, one step after the other. There were no shortcuts or easy ways, nowhere to hide. Gradually a clear sense of orientation returned to me and I knew where I was in the labyrinth. I walked the outer circle and the longest one.

At the fourth turn, I looked up and saw the yellow biplane disappear to the west; the buzzing engine sound faded away.

I placed my palms together on my chest. Then I slowly moved on. My mind became still and I perceived that nothing else needed to be done. Everything had been thought through; I had released everything that needed to go, so I could move on to the next level of my spiritual evolution. Lighthearted I approached the fifth turn and then the sixth.

A rush of energy surged through me. Something popped open inside my forehead, and I was surprised to realize that my perception of colors had intensified. The grass was greener, the sunrays shined brighter and the sky burst into bright blues. Enjoying my deepened perception, I considered that mystics tell us that we have two eyes that look into the outside world and a third eye, located in between our eyebrows, that looks within and reflects upon our inner processes. To me it felt as if my third eye had opened.

I moved on to the seventh path and felt comfortable and present in my body. Being naked out in nature has always connected me deeply to myself. I felt attractive and wholesome. In my family, there was no shame in being naked outdoors. Our isolated family farm offered the ideal setting to hose ourselves off with ice-cold well water on hot summer days, and my mother liked to do her gymnastic exercises naked in our garden. "The fresh air is good for your body and your mind," she said. My preference has been to swim naked in a lake or an ocean, if possible. I felt grateful for my healthy body and my physical strength, which allow me to handle my bike.

Then finally I took my last steps to the labyrinth's 14-foot goal area. A six-pointed copper star had been mounted above the center post. It symbolized the union of earth and sky, as well as the divine feminine and masculine energies that are present in all of us.

I had reached my own inner center and relaxed on one of the four benches. With my inner eye, I perceived myself in the middle of a vortex, rainbow-colored streams of energy swirled all around. The images transformed into an illuminated circular room, surrounded by movie screens. Each screen showed different scenes from my life, evolving clockwise according to my age. My new perspective as the observer revealed a deeper meaning. The interconnectedness of all events was evident.

The two screens to my right displayed unfamiliar pictures. I watched myself giving a presentation in an auditorium. Hundreds of people listened as I presented a slideshow about labyrinths. I exhibited diagrams and charts to describe the levels of awakening during a labyrinth walk. I connected the labyrinths, the chakras, and the seven levels in the Hebrew Tree of Life, as well as the corresponding organs in the human body. I showed data and scientific research to prove that the regular practice of walking labyrinths healed physical and mental diseases. Confident and strong, I was not the least bit intimidated by the huge audience. I looked mature, close to fifty. Dressed in professional attire and my long hair pulled back into a ponytail, I noticed dangling silver earrings with emerald and aqua stones. In my heart, I felt they were a gift from my mother. I witnessed a scene from my future and was in awe to see the possibilities in my life.

The second screen showed a man whom I loved deeply and me in an expansive garden, in what seemed to be the backyard of our house. The property was surrounded by large oak trees. The indigo evening sky displayed the first sparkling stars. Wood crackled as it burned in the fire pit and flames whispered into the night. Lightening bugs swarmed in circular upward motions above the 11-circuit Chartres replica that was laid out in the grass. The labyrinth emanated peace. The man and I relaxed in comfortable chairs and enjoyed a tranquil evening. I sensed that it wasn't Frank and felt a bit uneasy. Then the images vanished into the ether and I tried not to judge or analyze. I had seen a future filled with happiness and success. I didn't need to know how I would get there. I would see it soon enough as my life unfolded.

Then I opened my eyes, stood up, took a few deep breaths and retraced my steps out of the labyrinth. The tall prairie grass swayed to the gentle breeze and touched my skin. I was present in my body, aware of every step I took and at the same time my mind entered a timeless state; my past, present and future were one, existing simultaneously. A deep sense of trust and peace filled my heart. I returned to the labyrinth's entrance and got dressed. Carrying my boots I walked over to the Native American medicine wheel, located close to Toby's home.

10

The medicine wheel, like the labyrinth, demonstrates that life is a circle. Fourteen feet in diameter, this wheel was exactly the same size as the Prairie Labyrinth's center. Laid out with river rock on sand, it was divided into four equal parts, each of them representing a spiritual quality. The North symbolized the earth element, the West the water element, East the air element, and the South stood for the fire element. I sat down on the bench. My feet touched the sand, which tickled the soles. I lifted my right foot and gently massaged the reflex points. The understanding of these qualities is essential for me, as a holistic reflexologist, in order to analyze patients' feet and identify their needs.

The solid earth element is present in the heel; it represents people's ability to feel safe in their physical bodies. The flowing water element is located in the middle and soft part of the foot; here are the reflexes of the inner organs, revealing a person's level of emotional balance. The expansive fire element is found in the upper part and represents the ability to listen to one's heart and to be open to love. The light air element is located in the toes and shows people's yearning to develop their spiritual skills and to bring ideas from the upper worlds into the physical realm. The fifth element is the intangible realm of the ether.

The secret to living our fullest potential as human beings is to balance these elements and to embrace the continuous flow through the cycles of life, from spring to summer to fall to winter. I switched feet and massaged the left foot for equilibrium.

While gazing into the sand, my eyesight suddenly shifted. I closed my eyes, massaged my eyelids and opened them. The vision was still there. With eyes open, I saw thousands of tiny light specks dancing above the medicine wheel, coordinated by an invisible force and moving back and forth at high speed. Mesmerized I watched and quickly entered into an altered state of mind.

"Hello, Dorit, how are you?"

I heard Toby's voice and jolted back into waking consciousness. I took a moment to adjust while still perceiving the spectacle of dancing light. Accompanied by her dogs Toby approached the medicine wheel and sat next to me.

"Wow, I must have drifted off," I said, and the insights began to take clear shape in my mind.

During my vision, something amazing had happened. Only in retrospect did I realize that I had entered the fifth realm, the world of ideas or the ether, which exists outside the material world. It is the empty space that is omnipresent and everywhere. I was amazed to see the smallest components of matter, the atoms. I saw a nucleus of protons and electrons and the orbiting neutrons. No, I was not having a science class flashback; this was real; I saw it. It reminded me of planets circling around the sun.

The atom itself is composed of 99.9 percent empty space. The true basis of all matter is emptiness. Through our five senses we perceive the world we live in as solid, but I consider the possibility that it is only an illusion. Even the essence of a heavy block of iron is empty space. The cause of all creation originates in the ether, the realm of ideas. It makes sense to me that as human beings we are consciously able to choose to fill the void with either darkness or with light.

Toby and I shared a moment of silence. Then she turned her head, examined me with her wise green eyes and smiled.

"Very powerful" was all I could say, still processing the depth of my experience.

"So let's measure your energy field and see how it has changed," Toby suggested.

I got up and went to the same spot on her lawn where I had stood earlier. Toby walked farther and farther away from me. I laughed, "Toby, where are you going?" She reached the apple trees close to my parked motorcycle and turned.

"Wait and see," she said and took a few steps toward me. The L rods started swinging and then crossed. Toby came closer, counting every step.

"Seventy-eight feet," she said and arrived. We stood chest to chest.

"Incredible," I said. "I feel open, free, expansive, energized and a little bit lightheaded and here is the evidence. My field has grown by seventy-three feet."

"Yes it has," Toby said and then asked, "Are you hungry? I usually am starved after intensive spiritual experiences."

The thought of food caused my mouth to water, and my stomach grumbled.

"Yes," I said, and we walked over to the house.

I entered the hallway and Toby's original paintings filled the space with colorful splendor. I was impressed by a three by three foot acrylic painting in a robust oak frame. It depicted Toby standing in the center of a rainbow-colored chakra labyrinth. Her arms spread wide open to the heavens and she looked up to a golden eye in the sky. The pattern of a 7-circuit labyrinth spiraled through her body and above her crown.

"You are a gifted artist," I said. "It takes special talent to make the invisible world visible."

"Thank you," Toby said. We entered her kitchen and she opened her fridge. "I can make us egg salad sandwiches."

"That sounds great," I nodded.

Toby prepared the meal.

"How do you take care of your labyrinth?" I asked. "It must be a lot of work."

"The path is the exact width of my lawn mower, so I just drive through it. But as the prairie grass grows taller, I clip the fallen stems with pruning shears. This takes several weeks every fall. The prairie grass reaches its full height every two to three years, and then we burn it in a controlled fire."

We ate our sandwiches. Then Toby asked, "So, where does your itinerary take you from here?"

"I'll continue on through Kansas and my next invitation is in Boulder, Colorado."

"Good," Toby said. "There is a labyrinth in Boulder that you should experience. It is located at the Starhouse Community. I am involved in a project called the Art Line. Our vision is to create a line of walkable, interactive, outdoor artworks stretching across the heart of America on the 39th latitude. I didn't show you yet the earth pattern at the edge of the prairie. It is a 9-pointed star called Chante Esti, which means single eye of the heart. Chante Esti and the prairie grass labyrinth are part of the Art Line Project."

We finished our meal and then went outside. The dogs excitedly followed, jumping and barking, as we walked past the medicine wheel to a 55-foot design laid out in quartz crystal rocks.

Toby went on to tell me about her friend Alex Champion, a creator of earth art. Alex had helped her build this interlaced 9-pointed star according to a design adapted from one of Michelangelo's architectural achievements called 'The Campidoglio,' which once was the symbolic center of ancient Rome.

Chanti Esti's layout allows the seeker to choose the direction of their walk, either clockwise or counterclockwise through all the petals, and at any point, one may step right into the center. Herbs and flowers were planted on each of the island sections, and I rejoiced in an olfactory feast of lavender, sage, lemon, peppermint, rosemary and the dominant scent of blossoming roses.

"Toby, the roses are remarkable," I said, admiring her abundant lush blossoms of deep magenta, crimson and light red. "You know, my mother's rose garden on our farm is my most precious source of fond memories. I love watching my mom tending to her roses. She enters into a state of deep contemplation, as if nothing else exists. She doesn't even hear someone calling her, because she is completely absorbed in the care of her roses."

"I planted the roses to symbolize the universal energy of love," Toby said. "As you see, I placed the statue of Mary in the center to honor the Divine Feminine. Mary also represents the opening of the heart, which is needed to heal the old energy of fear and separation."

"It's fascinating. My mother's name is Maria, which is German for Mary."

"There are no coincidences; everything is connected," Toby said.

Silently we wandered the path of Chanti Esti and then, as if orchestrated by a higher force, Toby and I stepped into the center at the same instant.

A while later it was time for me to move on. We hugged and then walked over to my motorcycle. Toby quickly went to the studio and returned with her book.

"This is for you," she said and handed me *Keeper of the Circles*. She had written a dedication: 'Dorit – To a 'Field Connector' dedicated to connecting the grid and bringing the new energy to the planet – Light on the Path- Toby.' While I read the message, she picked apples from her trees.

"Take these with you, a gift from the earth for your nourishment."

I tucked the apples into my tank bag and then put on my jacket. Toby and I hugged one last time while Daisy, Sparky and Butch jumped up on my legs. Then I put on my helmet, turned the engine switch and my bike started with its powerful roar. Startled, the dogs barked violently and no longer recognized me as their friend. Toby called them back as I steered the Suzuki in a slow turn and headed to the road. Then I opened the throttle and accelerated quickly. In my rearview mirror, I watched the dogs chasing me.

11

Lonely country roads led from Toby's home to I-70. Then I sped off into the West. The scenery of the American heartland took me by surprise. Never before had I seen a green as lush and stimulating as the rolling hills that opened in front of me. I chased the sun underneath an endless sky. The Sunflower State was named after the river Kansas, which received its name from the Native American Kansa tribe that inhabited the area. The tribe's name is said to mean 'People of the Wind.'

I felt at home in this vast, abandoned landscape. My eyes focused on the farthest point on the endless horizon, my ears listened to the lulling hum of my engine and the wind whistled songs of the prairie into my helmet. It felt as if there was nothing else I would ever need in this world, only driving at a fast pace on a motorcycle in a primary-colored vision of green, sky blue and a bright sun-yellow.

A massive sheet of clouds from an incoming front up north rose into the sky, slicing it in half with the precision of a knife. Still mesmerized by the spectacle of the landscape, I was oblivious to the foreshadowed storm. Then hostile dark clouds closed in around the sun.

Immediately the temperature dropped and a chill ran down my spine. It became dark in an instant, as if someone had turned off a light switch. I had hoped to ride for another couple of hours and reach Russell, Kansas, but now I had to get off the road. The first raindrops sprinkled, and I exited at Salina to check into a Best Western.

I parked my bike in front of the hotel room and unloaded the bags. Two Harley Davidson motorcycles stood next to mine. The light sprinkle increased and a man in his fifties rushed to the Harleys. With quick, skilled movements he threw a rain cover on each bike. The many wrinkles around his eyes indicated that he might be the kind of guy who either gazed into the sun too much or laughed too often. The bikes were protected within minutes, and then he turned to me, big smile on his lips, and asked, "Traveling by yourself?"

"Yes."

"That's impressive." He walked around my bike and looked at my license plate. "Pennsylvania. Where are you headed?"

"California."

"Hm," he nodded. "My buddy and I are on our way home to Cincinnati from Sturgis. You know Sturgis, the world's largest motorcycle gathering in South Dakota?"

"Yes, I've heard of it."

"We go there every year. Our wives fly into Denver; they don't like these boring open roads," he waved his hand to the surrounding plains. "Together we ride the scenic roads through Colorado, spend a few days in Sturgis and then return. As a matter of fact, we just dropped off the wives at the airport this morning."

"The wives get bored? Well, I guess sitting on the back could get boring. I personally love the plains and the big sky," I said, untying my last piece of luggage.

"What's your accent?" He tilted his head, then guessed, "German?"

"Yes."

"Well, we're having dinner in a little bit. Would you like to join us?" he asked.

"Sure, I'll be happy to join. Beats having dinner by myself," I said, grateful for the invitation.

"Good. And by the way I am Elliott."

"Dorit."

"Dorit? Hm, That's a Hebrew name?

"Yes."

"Interesting." Elliott looked surprised. "Are you Jewish?"

"No."

"Well, I look forward to hearing your story; a non-Jewish German girl with a Hebrew name traveling on a motorcycle by herself through America. I bet that doesn't happen too often." His smile grew even bigger while he brushed the raindrops from his forehead.

"My friend's name is Barney. I'll knock at your door when we are ready to go."

Fifteen minutes later Elliott, Barney and I walked over to the truck stop, just a block away. Dark clouds raced low above the land. Trucks waited in line at the fuel station, blasting the deafening noise of their loud diesel engines.

"When you're on the road, the best food you can get is at a truck stop," Barney said.

He was a tall man with greying hair and gentle features. The hostess directed us to a booth. I sunk into the red-leathered seat, realizing my fatigue. The cold had crept into my bones, and I ordered a hot tea and a burger.

"So how long will you be on the road?" Elliott asked.

"Six weeks."

"Six weeks! That's a dream come true. I wish I could take off for that long. What do you do for a living?" Barney asked.

"I teach meditation and practice holistic reflexology."

"That must be a pretty good business," Barney said.

"Well, everyone needs to know how to relax. Stress is one of the major factors for many diseases. The ideal would be to live a balanced life and learn to prevent disease. But most people are too busy to take time for themselves."

"Isn't that the truth," Elliott said.

"Well, what do you guys do?" I asked.

"I am a dentist," Barney responded.

"And I am a PI," Elliott said.

"PI. What's a PI?" I asked. I had never heard this abbreviation before and was clueless about its meaning.

"Private investigator," Elliott smiled.

The waitress brought our beverages, and we continued to talk about the places we had traveled to. All of us had been to Brazil, and we agreed that Foz de Iguaçu, the waterfalls at the border to Uruguay and Argentina, were one of the most spectacular vistas to see. They also had been to Israel.

"I lived in Tel Aviv from '89 til '97," I said.

"No kidding," Elliot looked surprised. "My daughter was in Tel Aviv in 1991 during the Gulf War. She was twenty-two at the time and participated in a six-month program for the Israeli Defense Force, organized by a Jewish exchange program. My wife and I begged her to come home to the U.S., but she refused."

"Yes, I was in Tel Aviv. I can understand. I didn't want to leave either," I said.

Barney shook his head, "Why put yourself in danger?"

"Reality is different in Israel. It's a very small country, the size of New Jersey, surrounded by enemies. There is the constant threat of suicide bombers. It's part of your everyday life. And the Israelis were convinced that Saddam would not dare to attack, that it was impossible and that Tel Aviv was never attacked before," I said, holding the tea cup with both hands, trying to warm up.

"How did your parents react?" Elliott leaned closer, his brows furrowed.

"They wanted me to get out, but to me it felt like a betrayal if I would leave the country I had chosen to be my home and my Israeli friends who didn't have a different passport. They weren't getting out."

"You sound a lot like my daughter. She said the same thing," Elliott nodded.

"You weren't afraid?" Barney asked.

"No, not until the night of January 17, 1991. Well, I went through the mandatory training for a gas attack. I received my first gasmask and carried it everywhere. It was neatly packed in a carton box and had a long shoulder strap. The German Embassy demanded that all Germans evacuate Israel. But I didn't listen. My parents were terrified. They called several times a day, trying to convince me to get out. Then the airspace closed. My dad said to take a ferry from Haifa to Greece and come home. I made clear to him that Israel was my home and that I wasn't leaving. He was desperate; he yelled over the phone that I didn't know what war was. I didn't listen. After we hung up I painted the carton box of my gasmask, which looked kind of plain, with flowers and rainbows in red, purple, yellow and blue."

Both men shook their heads.

"Are you serious?" Elliott asked.

"Well, I was an art student." I shrugged my shoulders, "And of course, I had no idea what war was. My dad knew. He was born in 1929."

"And as a parent you want your children to be safe," Elliott pointed out.

"What happened next?" Barney asked.

"On January 17th the ultimatum was up. I shared an apartment with two other students. We cooked dinner and afterward everyone went to their rooms. I read and listened to music. Suddenly, my roommates stormed into the room, gasmasks in their hands and screaming: 'Bombs, bombs, we are under attack!'

I turned off the music and listened. A shrieking noise hissed through the air, followed by a deafening thump. It hit nearby. Quickly we put on the gasmasks and rain gear, which supposedly keeps the skin from melting in case of gas. We sealed the windows and door with plastic and tape. Gas is heavy and lingers at the ground, so we weren't allowed to go into the bunker. It was very hard to breathe with a gasmask on. They have a disgusting smell of rubber and you can't get enough air. I didn't know if I was inhaling gas. I grabbed the Atropine but my roommates suggested waiting with the injection until we felt sick or dizzy.

Then another missile hissed right above us and then another. We turned on the radio, desperate for news. But there were only reports of lightning and thunderstorms in Jerusalem. No mention of an attack. That is when it got scary, because you don't know if the next bomb hits your house and you don't know if you will be dead in a minute. It's crazy. Five hours later, sirens howled and the radio reporter gave the official announcement that Israel had been attacked."

"I can't imagine." Barney shook his head.

"Believe me, those were the longest hours in my life. We had a bucket to pee in. The room was sealed, so we couldn't get to the bathroom. When you're afraid, you pee all the time. I peed every fifteen minutes, everybody did. We were taking turns. I remember how my hands were shaking when I pulled my pants down. So awkward, gasmask on, rainjacket on, pants down."

"But then it wasn't a gas attack after all," Elliott said.

"Yes, thank God. The next morning everyone escaped from Tel Aviv. I went to stay with friends in Jerusalem. It was fairly safe there, assuming Iraq would not risk bombing the Islamic holy sites."

"Unbelievable," Barney said. His face had turned serious. "So many things we take for granted in this country. You truly realize that when you travel or hear stories like yours. I remember on my trip to Israel, I had to get used to the constant presence of armed soldiers. They are everywhere carrying their machine guns. And if you go to the mall or even a restaurant you get searched by security."

"Very true," I agreed.

The waitress brought our dinner.

"Could I please have some mayonnaise for my French fries?" I asked. She gave me a funny look and said she would be right back. Soon after, I happily dipped my fries into the mayonnaise. Barney and Elliott laughed at me. They laughed even more when I cut my burger with a knife and ate it with a fork.

"You are so typical German," Barney smiled.

"Well, we can never deny our roots." I didn't mind their amusement; it wasn't the first time people had commented on my condiment preference or how I ate burgers.

Elliott steered the conversation back to Israel and asked about my studies. I told him that I first went to Hebrew language school, then art school and then studied holistic medicine. I listed the many jobs I had held over the years to finance everything, since my parents didn't support the path I had chosen. But I also would not have taken their money. I needed to prove that I could do it my way.

"So what's up with your name?" Elliott asked. "Did you change it when you lived in Israel?"

"No, Dorit is my given name," I said. "I had no idea that it was a Hebrew name until I went backpacking in Brazil and met all these Israelis, and they told me it was a typical Israeli name."

"What inspired your parents to give you this name?" Barney asked.

"My mom picked the name. She doesn't recall what inspired her to call me Dorit. Nobody in Germany knew this name when I was growing up. I was always asked if it isn't Doris or Dorothy."

"So it was meant to be that you ended up in Israel," Elliott's face lit up with a big smile.

"I am sure. Imagine my surprise when I worked as a waitress in Tel Aviv and the first night, out of six waitresses, four of us were called Dorit. We were assigned numbers to keep our orders apart."

We continued to talk for a little longer, finished our meals and then returned to our hotel rooms, wishing each other safe travels.

I closed the door behind me, still thinking about our conversation. Sitting on the hotel bed I penned notes in my diary. The hidden remnants of one January night in Tel Aviv, in 1991, had stayed with me for a long time and continued to affect me. Five months after that night, I went to Germany for a visit. My mom and I were shopping for groceries at an outdoor farmers market. Suddenly a shrieking noise startled me. I froze, my breathing stopped, and then my body convulsed shivering. My mom looked at me worried. "Is everything all right?" she asked.

"Yes. For a moment the sound reminded me of the sirens during the Gulf War," I said. My mom shook her head silently.

I left Israel in 1997. Later during my first years in Pittsburgh I had lived close to a fire station. Every single time the sirens started, I felt a shock wave rushing through my body. Over time I gained control by focusing on deep abdominal breathing, which slowed my heart rate and stopped my body from shaking.

Now, fifteen years later, loud shrieking noises no longer cause a stress response. But without fail, the images still come back along with the memory of the distinct smell of a rubber gasmask. The hours when I didn't know if I was inhaling poisonous gas or air have been deeply embedded in my brain.

I left the diary pages open on the bed and took a hot shower. Afterward I read through my notes again. I had ridden exactly 333 miles. Earlier this day, Toby had pointed out the significance of numbers. In numerology, which I have studied, 333 would be seen as the number nine representing completion and mastery. Toby had chosen a 9-pointed star for her Chanti Esti design, instead of the original 12-pointed design by Michelangelo. She felt that this number would signify the completion of her earth art project.

I asked myself which circle in my life had come to completion this day but didn't come up with an answer. Outside, the storm unleashed its fury, and I fell asleep listening to the cracking of thunder and the bombardment of heavy rain.

12

On the fifth day of my journey, I woke up at 7:30 a.m. I opened the door and bright sunlight blinded me. I squinted and my eyes adjusted. A vast sky and white mountains of clouds towered above. Surprised, I noticed that the two Harleys were gone. 'I slept well,' I thought. I didn't even wake up to the roaring noise of their engines. My lungs inhaled the crisp, rejuvenating air. The earth had been washed clean, new and innocent. I was ready for another day of adventure. After two cups of coffee, plus bacon and eggs at the truck stop, I loaded my bike. The sky predicted a gorgeous day of riding, but I still put on the rain gear. The roads were wet and the spray swirled up by other vehicles would soak me.

I turned onto the highway and continued with good speed into the endless empty landscape. I didn't mind leaning into the strong side winds. I was uplifted and free.

Thousands of sunflowers smiled at the sun. The black tar stretched straight like a spine all the way to the horizon. I checked my speedometer and caught myself riding faster than the allowed speed limit. I was out in nowhere land, not much traffic, only a few cars and trucks, which I passed. My right index finger tipped the front brake, my precision machine reduced its tempo and the wind sang a different song into my helmet, a gentle, contained tune filled with the desire to soar forward.

Then Colorado welcomed me with the delightful speed limit of 75 miles per hour, ten miles faster than Kansas. Excited, I opened the throttle and a new song entered my helmet. The melody of the fast beat whirlwind of galloping horses chased me across the prairie.

Gradually the land turned to a flat, burned-out ochre. The sun had risen to its zenith and my bike needed fuel. I exited the highway and pulled into a service station, not too far from a community of single-story homes, isolated amidst the abandoned scenery. First, I took off my rain pants and stuffed them into an easy-to-reach luggage compartment. I filled the tank and then went into the store to grab some snacks. My regimen for long days of riding was to eat a hearty breakfast; throughout the day caffeine and sugar kept me going, and in the evening I liked a good meal and a cold beer.

The blonde kid behind the counter had been looking out the window, admiring my fully loaded bike. "You're going far?" he asked.

"I started in Pennsylvania. I am now on my way to San Francisco, then down the coast to Los Angeles, and through Arizona and New Mexico back to PA." I answered.

"Wow, quite a trip," he nodded impressed. "You gotta see my crotch-rocket," he said. "It's parked at the side of the building. I ain't going far though, back and forth to work, and the longest trip's maybe 50 miles. Nowhere to go around here," the kid said. He wasn't older than eighteen.

"Okay. I'll check it out."

I paid and went outside to take a look at his machine, a handsome blue Kawasaki Ninja. I found a spot in the sun, sat on the sidewalk and enjoyed my Coke and Snickers Bar. 'Crotch-rocket,' I thought to myself. 'What a funny word.' Testosterone-overloaded young men affectionately called their super sport bikes 'crotch-rockets.' There was no equivalent expression in my other languages - in German or Hebrew. People sometimes made remarks about my bike being a crotch-rocket, even though technically it isn't. The Bandit is a sport touring bike, with higher handlebars and more leg space for comfort. Considering that women are the fastest growing market, with 10 percent of motorcycles owned by female riders, maybe a more adequate expression is needed. But the only other term of endearment I came up with was 'tool for ultimate pleasure.' And still - one could interpret a double meaning.

Thrilled that I would see the Rocky Mountains in only a few hours, I hopped back on my bike and pressed on. The sunshine didn't hold. Like an omen forbidding me to witness the spectacular grandeur of the mountain range, black hostile clouds hovered at the horizon. Thirty minutes before I reached Denver, the traffic increased, signaling rush hour and the proximity of a big city. The scent of wet earth preceded the change in weather, and I stopped at the side of the highway to put on my rain gear. Cars sped by. Confined in their sealed boxes, the drivers were ignorant to the aroma of the earth when caressed by a light sprinkle. I filled my lungs with the fertile perfume of wild flowers and grass that lined the asphalt.

Fully protected, I merged back into traffic. The drizzle turned into a serious downpour and all romantic pleasantries of riding a motorcycle in the rain ceased instantly. I reduced my speed to stay safe. Water, splashed up by cars and trucks, made it hard to see and to be seen. I concentrated on the road map underneath the tank bag window and nearly missed the exit to bypass the city. The bike choked and cried for fuel. My left hand turned the reserve fuel switch.

The rain pounded harder adding to my misery. I pulled into a Boulder neighborhood with perfect lawns and single-story homes, relieved to be off the highway. Poor vision and the fog in my visor barely allowed me to read the street signs. I turned right at a traffic light, and a few blocks later I realized that I had taken a wrong turn. Suddenly the loud beeping of a horn startled me. A white sedan passed me and stopped sharply in front of me. A woman jumped out of the car. It was Jane. "Dorit, I am so glad you made it. Only one person in the world would be out in this weather on a motorcycle! Turn around and follow me; we are nearly home."

Jane sprinted back to her vehicle. Minutes later we pulled into a driveway, and she waved me into the garage. I parked the bike, took off my helmet and we hugged, water dripping from both of us. Drenched strands of short brown hair framed Jane's smiling face. In her early sixties, she emanated the unbound energies of a young girl, which she attributed to being a Gemini.

Her cheerfulness brought back the memories of our first meeting at 37,000 feet above the Atlantic Ocean. Sitting next to each other on an overnight flight from New York to Amsterdam, we both had been trying to catch some sleep, so it was only one hour before landing that we engaged in a conversation.

Jane was on her way to spend Christmas with her sister in Amsterdam before meeting up with friends in Tanzania, Africa. I was on my way to Germany and then would travel for New Years with my mom to Tenerife, Spain. After I mentioned the upcoming road trip, Jane immediately invited me for a visit.

Nine months later, we stood in her garage.

"I'll grab us towels." Jane disappeared into the house.

I took off my rain gear and the luggage rain covers, then unloaded the bike. Jane returned holding a bright green fluffy towel. I wiped off my face and the wet hair on the back of my neck.

"Let me show you to the guestroom," Jane said. "I'll take a quick shower and get changed."

The garage's entry way led into the kitchen. Tall windows displayed the view to a lush garden and nestled underneath aspen trees stood a family-sized igloo tent. Dark blue and black clouds rose above, emptying their heavy load of rain.

"I'll sleep out there tonight," Jane said as she pointed to the tent. "You will have the house to yourself."

"In this downpour?" I asked.

"It'll stop. The saying goes, 'If you don't like the weather in Colorado, wait five minutes.' During the summer I wouldn't want to miss a night to sleep outdoors. I love being in nature."

The guest room walls displayed framed photographs showing flowers, sunsets and galloping horses. I recognized Jane riding an athletic dark brown gelding. "This is Kahlua, my 24-year-old retired thoroughbred. Kahlua is sensitive and sweet. He is a real joy. I loved to show him in horse shows or just go trail riding to relax." She paused for a moment, gazing at the picture as if recalling happy memories.

"It's a nice looking horse," I said.

Jane nodded. "I made a reservation for a couple of horses. Did you bring your riding gear?"

"Yes, of course."

"Great," Jane responded and went off.

After I had carried in my luggage, I got comfortable on the living room sofa. Books were stacked on ceiling-high shelves. A volume on the coffee table caught my attention. The title read *Bhutan – Land of the Thunder Dragon*. Leafing through the pages, I was catapulted into a world of remote mountain villages high in the Himalayas, raging wild rivers gushing through untamed landscapes, white-tinted monasteries, monks with shaved heads and crimson robes and smiling people dressed in primary-colored festive local dress.

Showered and changed, Jane sat down next to me. "I visited Bhutan this spring," she said. "It's very unique. Westerners have sometimes commented on Bhutan's slow pace of development. The king says Gross National Happiness is more important than Gross National Product. Their culture is deeply based on Buddhist spiritual values of compassion and respect for all sentient beings. Their measure of success is the happiness of their people. There is so much we could learn from them. I became very interested in Buddhism after my visit; in a way it changed my life. I started to meditate every day and have tried to practice a Buddhist path of compassion, a clear and quiet mind and an open heart."

"Sounds like you went on a pilgrimage," I commented.

Jane nodded and I said, "In ancient times people only traveled for the purpose of pilgrimage. They embarked on a journey to sacred sites intending to reach a new level of spiritual development. Nowadays people travel more than ever in the outside world but often nothing changes within."

Jane agreed. "That's true," she said. "People try to escape their everyday life by living in the past or in the future. Travel is reduced to a means of getting away from hassles and responsibilities. But people can learn to be happy every day, by living in the present and connecting deeply with other people and with our beautiful planet."

In the evening we had dinner at Huckleberry's Restaurant, built in a funky old house in Louisville's Old Town, close to Boulder. On the way home Jane stopped to show me a local labyrinth built along the entrance road to a shopping mall. Jane thought this labyrinth, while well built, had not been located in the right space, being such a public and commercial location. She thought it wouldn't encourage the contemplative frame of mind and connection with the earth's energy, which labyrinths so often do.

River rocks lined the path of this 11-circuit Chartres design labyrinth. A grove of small cottonwoods moved gently in the evening breeze. Just recently built, the labyrinth felt young and immature. Slowly circling the labyrinth, I entered a meditative state and opened my kinesthetic perception to sense its energy field. I concluded, "The labyrinth will evolve. The more people walk it for meditation and prayer, the more powerful it will become. Sometimes it takes up to two years for a labyrinth to reach its full strength. At the same time, if a labyrinth is not walked, its power diminishes."

Jane looked surprised. "Interesting. I would not choose this place for a sacred experience."

"Of course, it's easier to connect to the sacred in pristine nature. But it is necessary to connect to the sacred wherever we are. I believe it's a good idea to place labyrinths in busy and public places. This helps transform negative energies and raises people's awareness beyond the mundane."

Tired from riding 490 miles in one day, I did not feel inspired to walk the labyrinth. We returned home. Smiling, Jane pointed to the star-sparkled indigo sky and then quickly disappeared into the tent.

13

Early the next morning, Jane and I went horseback riding at a local barn. We spent half an hour chasing two horses on foot around a huge pasture, both of them determined to let us get close and then galloping away laughing at us. Finally these two raggedly-trained horses allowed us to catch them. We rode out into the fields, with the Boulder Flatirons, Longs Peak, and the Continental Divide all on the horizon in the West.

I hadn't been on horseback the last couple of years. Feeling the movement of the horse underneath me brought back memories. My mind wandered to my youth when I was fifteen, the same year Silke had died.

It had been the season of fall storms, and one night I startled out of a dreamless sleep and opened my eyes to darkness. The loud, harsh cracking of tree branches screamed through the night. I heard a quick, loud knock on my door. The lights switched on, and my father rushed toward me, his green eyes flickering.

"Dorit, get up, hurry!"

I threw on jeans and a sweatshirt, ran to the entry room, pulled on my rubber boots, grabbed a warm jacket and raced to the barn. As a farm girl, I knew where to head in a storm. I leaned into the wind, fighting the gusts that tossed me sideways. Rain lashed into my face. I heard the heavy branch of a chestnut tree crashing onto the roof. In front of the illuminated entrance to the barn, shingles tumbled to the ground and burst into pieces.

My father, a tall man with black hair, a full beard and broad shoulders, guided my five-year-old silver-grey mare, Estella, out of the stable. His calm hand slid the bridle onto her head. Temperamentally, she pushed her nose forward. He instructed me: "The cows are in danger, and I am afraid they'll seek shelter beneath the poplars, which will snap like twigs in the storm. We have to find them and bring them home."

My father's strong arm lifted me onto the mare's bare back. "Trust your horse," he said. "Let the reins loose. Estella will guide you to the cows." He clapped my horse on the rear and we were off.

I felt the strength of my mare. I pressed my legs into her flanks, urging her forward. Darkness surrounded us. The wind pulled at my hair. Storm clouds raced across the sky. The thunder cracked and echoed over the plains of Germany's Lower Rhine Valley as I guided my horse toward the levee. Her secure steps on the muddy ground gave me confidence. I had never ridden her at night or in a storm, but I was not afraid. As we reached the top of the earth dam, I sensed the vast meadow that opened up in front of us. Lightning flashed, and for a moment the land around unfolded. The Rhine River, a silver stream, reflected the lightning. The poplars jerked back and forth to my far right. They were too distant to see the cows. Then everything returned to darkness. I heard my father's words, "Trust your horse. Let the reins loose."

I pushed my mare forward. I did not direct her where, but allowed her to find her own way. She moved slightly to the right and stepped carefully down the levee. I stroked and caressed her wet mane. Heavy rain poured down on us. I felt the rhythm of my breath synchronize with hers. I was strong and confident amid the fury of the fall season storm. We found the herd at the outermost edge of the meadow huddled underneath the poplars.

I called the cows, pressed Estella into a trot and clapped my hands. Thirty-five animals started moving. I sensed their nervousness. They lowed and moaned loudly. We moved up the levee and I heard tree branches snap. Lighting flashes revealed the silhouette of my father, racing toward us. He caught up, and together we brought the cows back home to safety.

While my father was securing the cows, I guided my horse into the barn, jumped off, and grabbed a towel to dry her fur. Estella turned her head, and I saw my dad enter the barn.

Then my father, a man who rarely showed emotion, looked into my eyes and said: "Good job."

I felt his love stream into my heart. I nodded, then turned and continued to dry off my horse.

I kept this memory to myself, not sharing it with Jane. I was too moved with emotion and felt grateful for my father, who had shaped me into the woman I had become.

Later that day we drove 15 miles southwest of Boulder to visit Nancy Franz, who had answered my call for outdoor labyrinths. A career coach by profession, she used her 7-circuit classical labyrinth to connect clients to their innate wisdom to find the right path. Protected by tall maples, aspens and silver Russian olives, her white farm house had been placed in between a graveyard and a school.

"That's a unique location," Jane said. "Like a cycle of life."

Nancy welcomed us. She was at ease, wearing short khaki pants, a pink T-shirt and sandals. Grey short hair framed her round friendly face. She opened her arms and hugged Jane and me. Her warm-hearted, sparkling personality felt contagious. "Thank you for being here. It's wonderful to meet you," she said. "Can I offer you a beverage, or would you like to walk the labyrinth first?"

Jane and I looked at each other and agreed to see the labyrinth. A paved walkway led around the house to an open pasture. Colorful river rocks in all shapes marked the sixty-foot labyrinth. I circled its diameter in silence. Then I returned to my two new friends who had been chatting. Expectantly, Nancy asked, "What does the labyrinth feel like?"

"Fertile, nourishing and full." I emphasized every word. "You must have had rich life-transforming experiences here."

"Yes," Nancy nodded. "Many transformations have happened here."

We prepared for our walk, the three of us standing in a circle at the labyrinth's entrance, holding hands and taking deep abdominal breaths. Then Nancy gave each of us a round smooth pebble. "Hold this during your journey. You may release your concerns and worries into the pebble or charge it with love. Find a special place for the stone and leave it as your offering. The labyrinth's force field will transmute all negative energies, creating a positive field of balance and peace."

Nancy looked at Jane, inviting her to enter the labyrinth.

"This is my first labyrinth walk. I've never done this before. I'll follow Dorit," she said.

I entered the labyrinth, allowing it to reveal itself to me and to change me. The sky displayed an impressive spectacle of high rising snow white cumulus clouds, competing with small, fast, dark and emerald blue clouds in a race from south to north. The sun, like a mischievous joker, appeared and disappeared, showing its face in between the ever-changing clouds. The rhythmic back and forth, inspired a stroll with easy-going, rejoicing steps.

My gaze focused from the heavens to the earth, drawing my awareness to the uniqueness of each river stone. One was round and soft like the skin of a baby. One was angular, rough and threatening with knife-sharp edges. Another one watched me with round dark eyes. The stones' colors varied from plain white, grey, and black to a musky yellow with the red stripes of iron deposits, meandering like thick veins in a wrinkled old woman's hand. Each stone was distinctive in its individuality.

My mind wandered to the many people I had met on my journeys. I had been inspired and enriched by every encounter, no matter how brief. Everyone contributed to who I was today. A blanket of warmth snuggled around my heart, and I was grateful for meeting Jane and Nancy. A short while ago we had been complete strangers, but here we shared the path as close friends. We were allies on this spiritual adventure, ready to bare our souls to each other.

The thought came to me that the essence of life is our ability to experience depth, honesty and unbound love in our human relationships. Unlike the accumulation of material possessions, these eternal values stay with us after our physical death. The Talmud, a collection of rabbinical debates and commentaries on the Old Testament, states that when we die, God and the angels weigh our hearts and measure our ability to love. Then either the gates of heaven will unlock or we will be forced back to earth, reincarnating into our next life, learning new lessons to purify and to open our hearts.

The rumbling roar of a freight train jolted me out of my contemplation. Slow paced, crawling at twenty miles per hour, it sneaked behind the graveyard. The earth trembled, a whistle blew and my mind jumped to a new subject. Orange bold letters spelled out the word 'Santa Fe' on the black locomotive's body. Santa Fe. Yes, I would be there in exactly one month, granted that all went as planned. Taking the straight road I could arrive in a day or two, but that would be as pointless as entering a labyrinth and walking directly to the center. Only by taking the long road, navigating through the twists and turns of life, could one evolve and learn.

A never-ending procession of railcars emerged behind the graveyard. The perpetual click clack of iron wheels drove like a sword into my consciousness and carried a disturbing thought. 'Would I be alive in a month?' In sync with my introspection, the sun vanished. A chilling breeze swiftly patted my skin. I lifted my head. The schoolyard across was deserted, devoid of all life.

Jane and Nancy followed closely, taking confident strides forward. I hesitated; my easy-going rejoicing steps turned careful and deliberate. I asked myself, 'Does any one of us know if we will be alive in a month.'

Startled, I moved forward to the labyrinth's center, the middle, also a symbol for the origin and final destination of our journey through life. 'Funny,' I thought, 'We are afraid to die but not scared of where we were before we were born.' Contemplating my origin calmed my mind. It felt like a peaceful place, benevolent and loving. My heart rate slowed and new oxygen streamed into my lungs. Breathing in and breathing out created the experience of duality. Breathing in requires tension and effort, breathing out moves us to relax and to let go. Unable to exist separately these opposites create one another. The moment we stop breathing we return to the center, a place of unity and our true origin.

The train passed, silence stretched out contentedly, birds sang and I entered the labyrinth's center. I placed the grey pebble that I had carried in my right palm close to an oval yellow-white rock; it looked like a small planet circling the sun. Awaiting Jane's and Nancy's arrivals, I enjoyed the present moment. Empty of thoughts, my mind was quite like the flattened surface of a lake, without a single ripple of disturbance. I moved clockwise within the center and then traced my steps back to the entrance.

Following the walk, the three of us sat on a bench overlooking the property.

"How long have you lived here?" I asked.

"Fifteen years," Nancy said and then continued. "It has been 30 years now that I set foot on this land for the first time. I came to sign a contract for a business transaction with the older couple that lived on the farm. The moment I entered the house, I had the eerie and overwhelming feeling that I would live here. It didn't make any sense at the time. Over the years I befriended the couple, and when they died they left the farm to me."

"You inherited the farm?" I asked.

"Yes. And another funny thing happened. Five years after I moved in I stood in the dining room overlooking the land, the same spot where I had received the intuition that I would live here, and a voice said, 'Build a labyrinth.' I couldn't deny the clarity of this guidance. Soon after, for my 50th birthday, I built the labyrinth together with six girlfriends."

"Where did you get the river rocks?" I asked.

"We collected them from the property," Nancy said.

"Those are a lot of rocks," I looked at her in disbelief.

"I know. I thought so, too. It was weird, as if the earth lifted the rocks out of the ground. My only explanation is that beneath the soil there may be an old riverbed. I don't know." Nancy shrugged her shoulders and turned to Jane asking how she liked her first labyrinth walk.

"It was a surprising experience," Jane said. "Walking barefoot at a slow pace helped me feel each part of my foot connecting with the warm earth. I thought about other people who had walked here and thought about absorbing their good intentions through my feet. But then I noticed that first I had to let go of my own negativity, which I wasn't even aware of. Thoughts came up from the past, painful events that happened many years ago. I released them through my feet. I felt bad and thought it would be too much. But the earth took it all in. The earth is very forgiving. After the release, I very easily concentrated on leaving my own thoughts of peace and freedom from fear, with each of my own steps. It felt very healing to me."

"The labyrinth is a wonderful healer," Nancy said. "Years ago I had a profound experience which still inspires me. I was going through a difficult time in my life; my heart was very hurt. At night I walked the labyrinth all by myself. I felt lonely and sad. I lay down in the center, and eventually it felt as if the rocks were singing lullabies to my heart. I was comforted and didn't want to leave. My life changed after that labyrinth walk. To this day I still hear the melody inside my heart."

We sat silently in awe, and then it was time for Jane and me to go. Thankful for Nancy's invitation, we hugged and said our goodbyes.

14

August 20, a Sunday. I hopped on my bike and headed toward the Starhouse Community, located on the 39th latitude near Boulder and part of the Art Line project. Toby Evans had recommended walking this labyrinth. Villas with abundantly colored flower gardens charmed me as I traveled up Mapleton Hill, a historic neighborhood. Delighted, I turned onto a winding road leading into the foothills. Mountain peaks rose up in the distance, their faces illuminated by the sun. The scent of pine streamed into my nostrils. I leaned into the smooth curves, flowing left, then right, and then left again, in perfect equilibrium with my machine. I could have traveled up this mountain road forever, but instead I came to an abrupt halt next to a prominent sign. Bold letters exclaimed:

Starhouse:

Visitors only allowed for events and classes.

NO TRESPASSING!

A dirt road led fifty yards straight up a steep hill. In the distance it zigzagged behind the pine forest and left me puzzled with the question of how much farther up it would go. I read the sign repeatedly, wondering how to proceed. I certainly didn't wish to intrude upon the community's privacy. At the same time I considered the dirt road's poor surface and its dangerous patches of gravel. Dark clouds loomed above. I had become accustomed to the continuously changing skies of Colorado. But if these clouds brought rain, it would transform the dirt road into a slick and treacherous trap, impossible to navigate on a motorbike. If I made the journey up, would I be able to come down later?

The engine idled impatiently. Pushing thoughts of worst-case scenarios out of my mind, I carefully opened the throttle. The bike ascended without hurry past potholes and loose sand as I made my way to the top of the hill. My new viewpoint opened to a grand spectacle of sky, mountains and the endless flatlands to the east, stretching out like a velvet carpet, dominated by vibrant green. The sky's mysterious teal and a tint of atmospheric purple and gold animated the landscape so that it appeared to be a living breathing being. Brilliant sunrays kissed the earth and a shiver of awe rose up my spine.

The ethereal colors brought tears to my eyes. My mind drifted back to a different place in time and space. I saw myself back on the farm in Germany as a young girl. Summer sunsets lasted until 11 o'clock, way past my bedtime. Punctually at 9:00 p.m. my mom tucked me in. Every night as she left the room, I sneaked to the open window, sat quietly on the ledge and watched the tender embrace of the night. First, the sky turned orange and then blood red, celebrating a last concerto before the sun dove off. Later, purple arrived and accompanied by a gentle and shy gold, paved the path for indigo.

Lulled by the perfumed air, rich with summer, I inhaled the heavy aroma of firs, dried grass and my mom's roses. Cows lowed as they dropped their heavy bodies, lying down in the meadow across the garden, their tails lazily brushing away the flies. Birds shrieked, startled by the sudden sprint of our dog, who wandered around the farm guarding his territory and now and then chased away a rabbit. On rare occasions, when the wind traveled northeast, I would hear the purring engines of ships passing through on the River Rhine.

For countless hours, I would watch the sky and listen to the sounds of nature. My ears were too busy identifying the voices of the night to perceive the one sound that was above all others. At first it approached me like a faint hum, shyly, coming from far away. Filled with wonderment I paid close attention and the hum grew stronger, as if my body fine-tuned its extra-sensory perception. And then one night, suddenly, whatever it was surrounded me and reverberated within my every cell. Comforting, rhythmic, slow-rising waves moved back and forth like the tides inside my body. I tried to synchronize my breath to the serene flow, but my lungs were too small to hold the amount of oxygen necessary. Weeks later it occurred to me that the source of this mystifying hum was the earth. I listened to the in and out breath of another living being. Overjoyed with this new discovery, I cherished my quiet solitary evening hours when I heard our planet breathe.

Then, protected in the temple of my youth, mesmerized by the gleaming aura of a nocturnal sky and a million bright-shining stars watching over me, I went to sleep and dreamed of traveling the world.

Music and laughter brought my thoughts back to the moment. A sign of life, the cheerful sounds of a party traveled from a house hidden behind trees. I felt the urge to speak with a community member and ask permission. As an uninvited guest, I was not sure if I had the right to be there. Toby's reassuring voice echoed inside my head, "You must walk this labyrinth."

Equipped with camera and tape recorder, I walked through an open field, following the arrows pointing to the Starhouse. The mountain sanctuary, a twelve-sided stone building with a roof floating like a wave, stood harmoniously surrounded by monoliths. Toby had mentioned that this sacred space was dedicated to spiritual and ceremonial practices, based on love of the Divine, honor for all beings, earth stewardship and community celebration.

No signs guided me to the labyrinth. A grove of pine trees, though, attracted my attention, and I followed the hint. Suddenly a familiar 'click' jolted through my body, like a key turning a lock. I had felt this shiver before, miles before reaching Toby's prairie labyrinth. The tree grove opened like a secret chamber, sealing it from all outside noise. I found myself in complete silence as I stepped in. Nestled in between pine trees the 7-circuit classical labyrinth spread out with grace and beauty. Overgrown with yellow wildflowers, sage and rosemary, stacks of rocks outlined the pattern. I inhaled the scent of herbs and pine. The sky had turned steel grey and hovered dense with anticipation. I took off my boots and socks.

Barefoot, I embarked into the labyrinth. Warm sand touched the soles of my feet, and I steadily circled toward the core. Clean air streamed into my lungs; a calm heartbeat brought serenity and relaxation. The fourth turn took me by surprise. A furry black spider, the size of my palm, viciously attacked an insect with pretty red markings. I nearly crushed both underneath my feet. Shocked, I jumped back. My heart raced; all inner peace evaporated.

'Everything in the labyrinth is a metaphor,' I thought. The black spider jerked the insect that desperately tried to break free, moving its tiny legs in vain. This was a sign. Appalled, I turned and took a few steps back, determined to leave.

An authoritative force stopped me. "You are not getting out of here," it said. My escape route was blocked. Startled, I took a few deep breaths, trying to calm myself. Once before, at the labyrinth in New Harmony, Indiana, I ran into a wall. Then I couldn't get in; this time I couldn't get out. I made one last futile attempt and was jolted back.

Rationalizing, I convinced myself that this was a spiritual learning experience and there was a reason for this strange occurrence. A sharp pain firmly gripped my stomach. Pressing my thumbs into my solar plexus, I attempted to open the knot. Thoughts stormed into my mind, like soldiers invading sacred territory. The onset of this debacle started with the 'No Trespassing' sign. Instantly my mind was split in half between 'Yes' and 'No,' between 'entering' and 'not entering.' Each further action would result in consequences that I couldn't foresee. 'Ah, the human dilemma of free choice,' I pondered. I had to face myself and continue on this journey that I had chosen. The spider killed the insect. Which inner conflict was played out? Cautiously I moved forward, deeper into the labyrinth, deeper into the mystery of my own soul. 'No Trespassing' the sign had said. Easily I could have turned around and obeyed the rules. But something told me not to, told me to climb the hill, take the risk and enter uncharted territory. Unable to escape my true calling, I struggled against my upbringing of strict German obedience, a mentality that demanded I stick to the rules, not dare too much, play it safe. The German side of me I saw clearly in my own life, in my need for order, to have a plan, to be well organized. Was this the same German obedience that birthed servitude, allowing small-minded people to fulfill their orders, without questioning, to feel innocent, while committing horrendous atrocities?

Instantly I felt catapulted back to Israel. Shortly after my arrival, I had taken a bus and sat next to a man in his seventies. He wore a short-sleeved shirt. My gaze had drifted toward the window and then suddenly froze. I stared at the man's arm. Numbers were tattooed on his wrinkled skin. The man nodded, looked into my eyes and gave me a friendly smile. This first encounter with a Holocaust survivor was unforgettable. In my mind I recalled his clear blue eyes and still wondered what horrors they had seen. During my years in Israel, I saw many more blue-inked numbers, etched with meticulous precision into human skin.

I journeyed deeper into the labyrinth, deeper into my soul. I felt a strong reassurance that if I kept questioning the answer would emerge. I walked briskly and found peace by being in motion. The solution was already there; I had to evolve spiritually to find it. Looking back on my life, I knew that every problem I had ever faced was an invitation for growth and change.

A book that I had read at nineteen came to mind. The Native American author wrote about the responsibility of the white man for the future of our planet. In my favorite passage we were called to act consciously and conscientiously. The deeds of our generation would affect the next seven generations in a positive or negative way.

As a German, being removed two generations from the atrocities, I felt the effects on my generation in the form of guilt, denial and shame. No matter how far I traveled, this was an inescapable part of my identity.

The eighth turn carried me to the labyrinth's center.

An image emerged in front of my mind's eye. I saw the reconciliation labyrinth in South Africa. Two entrances open to two separate paths, which spiral to one center. A metaphor for life, the South African labyrinth is a shining beacon symbolizing unity and oneness of all. We all have originated from the same source and will return to the same source. No matter how far we have felt separated from our fellow human beings, it is our responsibility to reconcile, to create a different future for us and for the generations to come.

Lost parts of my own soul mended together, I felt as if a huge burden had lifted. My chest opened, I breathed freely and the knot in my stomach dissolved. I thought, 'If I can be at peace, I am able to create a reality of peace for myself and my immediate environment.' The door, which had been locked tightly, opened and revealed a new beautiful vision, millions of people at peace with themselves manifesting a new reality of global peace. 'Change happens one person at a time,' I thought, 'One footstep at a time, as we journey deeper into the labyrinth.' The vision of hope filled my heart and in-sync with my inner process the sky opened and gentle sunrays transformed the labyrinth. A bronze glimmer illuminated the rocks; for a moment they looked like the crusted skin of a prehistoric being. I kneeled and bowed in front of my destiny, in agreement with whatever it may bring. Then I retraced my steps out of the labyrinth and never again saw the spider or the insect. I bowed one more time at the labyrinth entrance, thanking the forces that had brought me there. Sensing my connection to the source, a strong tingling sensation stimulated the crown of my head. I wondered how far my energy field extended. Toby's dowsing rods had measured my aura after I walked the Prairie Labyrinth. I had been surprised then, but this time I guessed my field extended even further. Enriched, clear, expansive and free of burden, I walked back to my bike.

15

Monday, August 21, the eighth day of my journey. I merged into morning traffic heading toward the Rocky Mountain National Park. The air was crisp and I felt excited because the top of the world awaited me. I passed cars and looked at the expressionless faces of people on their way to work. I realized the magnitude of events that happened in only one week. I was a new person and felt as if all cords to my old life had been severed. If time were measured in digits of quality instead of quantity, my quality curve would have peaked with pleasure every moment, every day.

Estes Park, the doorway to Trail Ridge Road, welcomed me with its souvenir shops and Bavarian style architecture. I fueled up one last time and got back onto the main street following two motorcyclists on Beemers. They raised their hands and waved. Cheerful, I returned the universal greeting among motorcyclists.

At the park entrance booth I again met the two bikers. I drove off first, only to pull off the road a few miles later taking pictures of green rolling hills, which rose to distant skyrocketing snow-covered peaks and brilliant skies. The bikers passed me, waving again. Farther up, I overtook them while they photographed scenic views. We played this game a couple more times until I lost sight of them.

My solitary ride up the mountains brought an ecstatic sense of alertness. My heart beat faster in the face of these majestic landscapes. I felt big and small at the same time. Big, in the face of my adventure. Strong and confident that I was living my dream. Yet, I felt small, contemplating that

I am one little person, easy to get lost in this vast scenery. I sensed that life creates itself out of opposites. Grinding inner forces push together to catapult us to new peak experiences.

The constant purr of my machine kept me in the moment. The road snaked higher and higher and every turn brought a new surprise. Pressed into the shadow of a steep rocky wall, covered by a haze of foggy moist air, the next curve spit me out into bright light and the sight of lush green valleys and giant naked ridges. I looked back on the path I had traveled. Pearl-sized cars hung on a necklace of road circling around the mountain. The next turn brought a new sky, a bright cerulean blue, dotted with cotton balls, casting playful, quickly moving shadows on the land. Minutes later, the sweet white puffs had grown into high rising cumulus clouds, which broke the sunlight into rays of rainbow colored orange, yellow and turquoise.

The next curve straightened out into a steep climb along the grim face of the mountain. A cliff hundreds of feet deep lurked to my right. A sudden gush of wind pulled me first left and then jerked me to the right. I gripped the bike's handles, balancing against the current. All temptation to watch the mind-boggling vistas and the razor-sharp mountain edges ceased. Trembling, I didn't dare turn my head. I rode close to the center line. My gaze focused on the tarmac ahead, expecting the next blow of wind that could easily sweep me off the mountain. My heart raced, but there was no time for fear. I had to stay centered and shifted down into second gear while breathing from my abdomen. The gust picked up, trying to throw me off balance, but prepared, I leaned my bike into the stream.

'Funny' I thought, 'A year prior I had traveled through the Shenandoah National Park on Skyline Drive in Virginia.' Gentle sloping grades climbed to 4,000 feet. Rustic stone walls and guardrails fenced the road, protecting the driver from swerving over the edge into danger.

Skyline Drive had been harmless and risk-free, compared with the Rockies' Trail Ridge Road which was devoid of these safety precautions.

Temperatures plunged as I ascended above the tree line. A freezing chill ran through my body. Aware that hypothermia presented a real threat to motorcyclists, reducing the ability to judge and respond quickly, I began to meditate. My awareness focused on the base of my spine, visualizing a radiant ball of energy. While flexing my pelvic floor muscles, a stream of warmth shot up my spinal column and distributed heat throughout my entire body. Minutes later I was comfortable and relaxed. This technique had proven its practicality on many cold weather riding days.

Exposed on an open emerald green plateau, the bike leaned into the strong side winds. The sky displayed a dramatic race of dark heavy clouds, storming across the cold blue sky. The sun flashed its last light onto the barren crests and then vanished behind the distant storm front, turning the world pale and colorless. Temperatures plummeted. I kept going, navigating around a bend. Suddenly, as if rushed by an invisible master, the storm stood right in front of me, hurling heavy drops of rain at me. Cracking thunder echoed all around, lightning flashed viciously. Quickly I pulled to the side of the road, grabbed my rain gear and slipped into my protective jacket and pants. Confident about soon reaching the alpine visitor center, 12,183 feet above sea level, I rode on.

The weather closed in, like an enemy circling its prey. The rain turned into hail, hammering like deafening cannonballs onto my helmet. I could barely see. My fingers froze inside my soaking wet leather gloves. No matter how much I tried to meditate myself out of this predicament, it was impossible to stay warm.

Then out of a hostile wall of storm emerged the two motorcyclists, explicitly demonstrating a cut throat sign, signaling me to follow them. I turned. The back tire slipped on the slick asphalt and only pure luck allowed me to regain balance. Two miles down the mountain, we left the bikes next to a shelter and huddled underneath a tiny roof, barely protected from the pounding hail.

"Out here by yourself?" one biker asked. We kept our helmets on. All I saw were his friendly hazel eyes.

"Yes," I nodded.

"Well, it gets hazardous out here. I was worried the hail would turn into ball bearings, and then we would have been sliding all over the place."

"I thought I would make it to the visitor center and take a break there." Both men shook their heads. "No, you would not have made it."

Knowing in my heart that I would have attempted to rough it out, I said, "I am glad you were ahead of me. I would not have given up and probably would have gotten myself into trouble."

Shivering from the cold, I shook my arms and legs to get my blood circulating. I took off the useless frozen gloves. My insulated rainproof winter gloves had stayed at home in Pennsylvania. I had not even considered packing them. 'Well, we learn from our mistakes,' I thought.

My rescuers were Zigy, a photographer from Boulder, and his buddy Dan, a paramedic from Austin, Texas, on his BMW K 1200RS. Equipped with Gerbing heated motorcycle jackets, their only complaint was the hail. Zigy's black BMW R 1150 GS featured heated grips to warm his hands. Half an hour later the sky cleared. Again I was baffled by the illusion of distances. Surprised by the storm's hasty assault, I saw within minutes the dark clouds disappear behind high peaks not leaving a single reminder of the previous threat. We swung back in the saddle and journeyed to the summit.

Steam rose from the asphalt. Under the glistening sun, moisture evaporated quickly. Without effort we reached the crowded alpine visitor center, parked our machines and took off the heavy gear.

Dan replaced his helmet with a baseball cap. He had a stocky, muscular stature, dark hair, a cute mustache, and the inscription on his black shirt read, 'I didn't know that BMW made cars until I passed one.' Zigy was a tall, nice-looking man with a weathered face and short brown hair. His eyes twinkled mischievously. Well-traveled, he was the kind of person who knew how to enjoy life. His father was Russian, his mother Hungarian; born in Italy, he stated, "I am not your typical American."

Passing the touristy souvenir shops, I got in line at the snack shop. My long wait was rewarded with a sandwich and a hot chocolate. I warmed my hands holding the hot cup until life returned to my fingers. Zigy brought coffee and sat next to me.

"Hey Dan, do you want to keep going 'til Grand Lake Lodge? We could accompany Dorit a little farther," he asked.

Dan didn't hesitate. "Yes, of course. Great idea," he said.

"That's awesome. Thank you, guys." I smiled, happy about their company.

Rejuvenated by our break, we took the obligatory pictures with the grand mountain views and then returned to our bikes.

The descent was an easy-going cruise. The steep winding curves turned into long straight stretches and Zigy, our front man, waved me to drive closer. Clueless about his intention, I opened the throttle to catch up and then realized that he was taking photographs while navigating his BMW motorcycle. The cord strapped around his neck, he operated the camera with one hand. Impressed with his ability to multi-task, I gave him the thumbs up.

Grand Lake Lodge, a historic resort, offered a spectacular view of the rich cobalt blue Grand Lake and surrounding pine forests and mountains. We got comfortable on the front porch's wooden bench and spent relaxing moments together before our final goodbye.

A grey-haired gentleman in his early sixties approached us. "I saw you arriving on your motorcycles. Could I ask you a question?" Unanimously we said, "Yes."

"My wife and I are visiting from Dallas, Texas; I just got my motorcycle license a year ago and had planned to ride Trail Ridge Road together with my wife on a brand new Harley Softail. We drove up in our camper, and it was very intimidating. Actually, I can't even imagine riding up on a motorcycle. It would freak me out; it's scary. Did you ride Trail Ridge Road?"

We nodded.

"Weren't you terrified?" he asked.

"Sometimes," I responded. "We ended up in a hailstorm; that wasn't very pleasant."

"Well you know, Trail Ridge Road can be treacherous, but the three of us are experienced riders," Zigy said. "Our bikes are built for sport touring; they aren't as heavy as your Harley. And we don't carry passengers. It is admirable that you have the courage to say 'No' and to know your limits. Get a few more years of riding experience under your belt before you try to master Trail Ridge Road."

"Thank you. I appreciate your advice," the man said and then engaged in a conversation with fellow Texan Dan. Afterward we returned to our machines, hugged, promised to stay in touch, and then drove off in different directions.

My journey continued on scenic Route 40 into Steamboat Springs. Ski lifts looked like misplaced skeletons on the backdrop of green hillsides. From the chilling heights of the Rockies, I had transitioned to 93 degree heat. Vacationers populated street cafés and restaurants. I drove slowly, enjoying the music and laughter that traveled to my ears. Late in the day, at

6:00 p.m., I still felt eager to keep going. 'Why wait till tomorrow, if I can do it today,' I thought, pulling into a parking lot. A look at the itinerary revealed a small dot some 45 miles ahead. Knowing that these tiny specks sometimes represent a handful of rundown homes, lacking accommodations for travelers, I asked a woman walking her collie. Helpfully, she leaned over the map and said, "Well, if you only need a hotel and dinner, keep going. But there is nothing else."

Back on the road the change of landscape mesmerized me, turning dry and flat, illumined by golden rays of setting sun. Forty-five minutes later I arrived in Craig, located in Colorado's high plains and home to eight thousand souls. I shot right through the main street to the exit of town, surprised to find three large hotels. I parked in front of the Best Western and headed to the check-in.

"We're completely booked," the clerk informed me gravely. "The Super 8 as well. If you are fortunate you may find a room in the Holiday Inn." I rushed to the Holiday Inn and got in line behind a dozen sweaty men, wearing work clothes and heavy boots. My turn came. The lady behind the counter asked for my reservation number. I shook my head and she frowned.

"Let me check the system; we may have a room or two left," she said.

"Why is it so busy?" I wondered.

"Miners! We are booked for weeks at a time," she explained. The tone in her voice implied that I should have known this important fact. Minutes later she saved me by locating a suite. I was happy to take it at $130 a night, priced far above my budget.

Hungry, after unloading the bike, I looked forward to a good dinner. The bar featured a number of television screens, offering a nice distraction for a lonely traveler. But crammed with more than 30 beer-drinking men it was not a place for a single woman. I opted for a solitary meal in the deserted dining room. Later, after a hot shower, I went to bed exhausted from an eventful 279 mile day. I fell asleep to the noise of a TV in the next room.

16

Awakened too early at 6:30 a.m., I cursed my loud neighbors in a very non-enlightened way, as they robbed me of my sleep. 'Who would blast the news channel that early in the morning?' I thought. 'With no good news ever, why listen to it at all? Why ruin an entirely perfect day?' I put the pillow over my head, but awake and annoyed, I couldn't return to my dreams.

By 8:00 a.m. I was back on the road, still sensing the delicious taste of strong coffee on my lips. The warm wind streamed onto my face through the slightly open visor. I stood up on my foot pegs, stretching my legs at 60 miles an hour, then got comfortable on my seat, opened the throttle and sped off into a new day.

I overtook a handful of trucks and cars and then left civilization behind. Uninhabited spaciousness took me into its loving embrace. I didn't see another vehicle, truck, settlement, farm, person or animal. Nothing, there was nothing, only the burned-out ochre landscape rolling to the end of the horizon. Straw-colored grass waved defiantly despite its thirst. Bushes swayed wildly torn by the wind. The endless azure sky watched in silence while the straight black tarmac led west, and the illusion of water shimmered on the asphalt in the morning heat.

I rode for an hour in solitude, then released my grip on the throttle, and the bike surrendered to a stop. I turned off the engine, opened the zipper to my luggage and grabbed the Pentax. My camera was nothing fancy or modern, not even digital. For me, memories from far away places,

Australia, Israel, Germany and Spain, resided in its dark interior, making it impossible for me to replace it with a newer model. Every time I took a photograph, a yearning stirred my heart, reminding me of love, pain and a good life lived.

I directed the zoom to capture the landscape. 'Ah', I thought, 'How can justice be done to this remarkable moment in time and space? How can the endless, the limitless be confined into a small framed four by six photograph?' Despite this I took a handful of pictures and proved it a futile attempt.

I stepped into the center of the road, opened my arms wide and spun 360 degrees around my own axis. I inhaled deeply, filling my lungs with the scenery's mystical charisma. My heart pumped oxygen-rich new blood to every cell, and the moment was captured within me.

Light and expansive, I stepped back to my bike and noticed a small animal's scattered white bleached bones. Studying the skeleton, I wondered about the fate of what could have been a young deer. Vertebras rested on the dry earth that had cracked from lack of water. Tibias and femurs spread on brown wilted grass. The ribs, detached from the spine, lay side by side, next to a yellow-leaved thorn bush. The skull was gone. The remains weren't threatening or hostile; they looked peaceful, carefully arranged by time and wind. I saw them as a reminder that the essence of our existence cannot be found in the physical. Our fragile, perishable bodies are not who we are. We are the sum of fleeting moments that belong to us for eternity. It is our choice and responsibility to create moments of beauty and grace, instead of despair and suffering.

My soul stripped bare to the bone and my mind emptied of unnecessary thoughts, I continued to travel west.

A road sign displayed a ski jumper conquering the sky, triumphing high above snow-covered mountains. Crimson letters read: Welcome to Utah. The barren landscape created an intoxicating effect on my psyche. I was spellbound. Coming from Europe, where land is precious and overpopulated, I had never witnessed the enchantment of empty space. The town of Jensen and the Green River blinked like emerald diamonds in the distance and marked my return to civilization. Disappointment ached inside my heart as I descended from the plateau of crusted scorched earth.

Throughout those past hours I had fallen in love with vast, lonesome and empty spaces.

Close to Salt Lake City, before merging onto I-80, I stopped to fuel up and pulled alongside two Harleys. The friendly bikers immediately engaged me in a conversation. They were a team of a father, dressed in leathers, with tattooed arms and greying black hair in a ponytail, and a well-shaven son, who looked like a businessman and not a biker, in khaki pants, a button up shirt and short brown hair, and the son's pretty wife. Traveling from Seattle, Washington, visiting the Rocky Mountain National Park, they were headed to Lake Tahoe for a family reunion.

"I loved Route 40," I said, still feeling the vibration of the land resonating inside my body.

"We couldn't wait to get out of Colorado," the father said.

"Why?" I was surprised.

"We were just having a good ole time until we passed a van; you know the good Christian family with the holy Jesus fish. They must have been afraid of bikers and called the cops on us," he said.

"Ten miles later we were stopped by two police cars, and they treated us as if we were the worst criminals," the son continued, "Warning us not to be seen again. They didn't have anything on us; all we did was a little speeding. But there are people in this world who live in fear, and they feel threatened by anybody who is different."

"Live and let live is my philosophy," the father said. "I don't bother you and you don't bother me. It's that simple."

Amazed about our opposite experiences, I shared my itinerary.

"We're heading the same direction. Would you like to join us?" the father suggested. "Then you don't have to cross the Salt Lake by yourself."

"Thank you, but you guys are ready to leave, and I'd like to take a little break, call my mom in Germany and fuel up." Without further thought I dismissed their offer. We wished each other good travels; then they started their machines and took off.

I purchased my regular fix of a Coke and a Snickers bar, sat underneath a sun umbrella, considered the eight hour time difference across the Atlantic Ocean and called my mom. She promptly answered, and I was happy to hear her familiar voice.

"I knew you would call soon," she said, confirming our telepathic connection. She had stayed close to the phone, expecting to hear from me. Despite living in the 21st century, my mother refused to get an answering machine or a portable phone. "If people need to reach me they know where I am," she said. Her attitude translated into an open invitation for anybody who wanted to stop by at the farm. My mom loves to serve a cup of coffee or sweet berry liquor, welcoming the guest for a chat.

Years ago I bought her an answering machine, but she passed it on to a friend. Like her, I was stubborn when Frank had bought me a cell phone for my trip. "Payphones are just fine," I said, feeling that being reachable would interfere with my intention to detach from everyday life.

"Just take it," he insisted. "You may need it when you get into trouble."

"I am not getting into trouble," I said. But still, I took the phone.

My mom listened to my previous day's adventure and the description of Trail Ridge Road; although I carefully edited out the threatening hailstorm.

Attentively she picked up on the quality of silence between the words and asked, "So everything is going well?"

"Yes."

"Be careful."

"Always, mom."

We hung up. I held on to the phone for a minute, trying to grab something stable, like a long gone memory from my childhood. The echoing sound of static signaled that it was time to move on.

The interstate took me through Salt Lake City and spit me into a glistening basin of pure white, a shining surface, surrounded by mountain ranges in the far distance. The desolate wasteland of the Great Salt Lake Desert burned like a furnace. At 110 degrees, sweat streamed out of my pores, trickling down the inside of my jacket. My lungs rejected the overpowering odor of sulphur and heat that burned inside my nostrils. It was difficult to breathe. A sign read, 60 miles no services. At 90 miles per hour I was going with the flow of traffic. People in air-conditioned cars stared at me, the only motorcyclist out in this hostile environment. 'What did I get myself into?' I thought. The perfect heartbeat of my bike's engine soothed my nerves. The steady, reliable sound was my constant companion on this journey. Suddenly the melody changed and a whistling whine disturbed my peace. My thoughts raced. 'What's wrong?' I questioned. The air-cooled engine struggled and gasped, but still kept going at a good speed.

The high-pitched whine increased, shrieking into my consciousness, and brought bad thoughts. I saw my bike breaking down, saw myself stranded without help. Worried, I felt sure I had reached the end of my voyage. My mind wrapped itself around the image of failure. There was nothing else I could see. I accepted the fact that my engine would give up its spirit any minute. Saddened by a wave of regret, I counted all the things I wouldn't do as tears filled my eyes. I would not reach the West Coast, not meet up with my friend Erin in San Francisco, not ride Highway 101 along the Pacific Ocean, and not reunite with Frank to figure out the details for the next chapter of our lives in Southern California. I would not accomplish what I had promised to do. A total disappointment, I would not reach the frontier that I had set for myself. I waited for my engine to die.

It must have been the heat, or the lack of oxygen rich air, free of sulphur, that had brought the sluggishness of thinking. All of a sudden I realized what I was doing. I had allowed negative thoughts to flood my mind creating a reality of destruction and failure. If I wanted the engine to die, I would just have to visualize it. The manifestation in the physical realm would follow with the certainty of a self-fulfilling prophecy. Thoughts govern matter. As a meditation teacher, I should have known better. I instructed my students to focus their thoughts single-mindedly on the reality they desired. Their lives changed in extraordinary ways, and here I found myself trapped by negative self-talk.

Sorting my thoughts, I allowed only positive visions to enter my head. I saw myself rejoicing as I rode my perfect machine along the Pacific Ocean. I felt the awe of walking the labyrinth at Grace Cathedral and the happiness my friend Erin and I would share, spending four days together. The negative clutter dissolved. It is simple; when we shine the light into the shadow, the shadow turns into light.

The engine's persistent whine remained my only nuisance. Seeking a new sound, I began chanting OM. Based on Indian philosophy, the Sanskrit word OM is the sacred sound that calls the universe into existence. A sound above all sounds, beyond past, present and future, it is the supreme name of God. Physically it is related to the third eye located in between our eyebrows. It is said that we have two eyes gazing into the physical world and one eye that looks within in order to reflect upon our inner processes, asking why things happen the way they happen and seeking meaning in our existence. Our blindness disappears when the third eye opens. Only when we look within, can we truly see. Interestingly, the pituitary gland and hypothalamus are located behind our third eye at the base of the brain. These organs are related to the supervision of bodily functions at the highest level. Chanting the sacred OM balances our hormone system.

The deep sound resonated on the roof of my mouth traveling to my brain. My thoughts slowed down, tamed from a wild destructive gallop to a smooth focused trot, and positive visions dominated my mind. The sound reverberated within me and all around in the closed space of my helmet, intensifying its positive effect on my psyche. I relaxed and the heat didn't bother me any longer. My excessive sweating represented the release of toxins from my body, as well as the toxic thoughts from my mind.

Entering a state of a natural high, I saw myself traversing an ocean of bliss. Purged and purified I arrived in Wendover, fueled up, gulped down two bottles of water and then continued into Nevada.

17

The engine sound didn't ease, but the bike rode on with full power. The whine expressed its complaint about the heat and the altitude. Unsurprisingly, I had started talking to my machine as if it were a person. Not any person, but a strong, determined woman. I encouraged her, saying: "You are brave. You'll never give up. Show me what you can do. Show me how capable you are. Keep going for me, please." I petted the metal tank, like a horse's neck. Laughing at myself, I knew that I was not delirious, but clear-minded. A natural result of solitary travel, my machine became an extension of myself.

People had asked me, before this trip, if my motorcycle had a name. I had considered the question to be absurd; machines don't have personalities, even though Frank called his FZ 1 his mistress and cared for her with tender love. I had to admit, to me, the nickname was not funny since Frank was very flirtatious with other women. My friend Karin, in Australia, had named her red '84 Ford Telstar Gaia. Five years ago, I visited her in Melbourne, and we embarked on a trip to Tasmania. The stubborn car regularly refused to start. Karin patted the dashboard and said determinedly, "Come on Gaia, you can do it." And seconds later the magic words inspired her car to jump to life. If my bike had a soul, it clearly would be female and content with its given name, Bandit.

One hundred eleven miles later the sun cast long shadows, and it was time to get off the road. I pulled into Elko and took a room in the High

Desert Inn. While waiting at the check-in, a man in his early thirties dressed casually in jeans and T-shirt examined my loaded motorcycle parked at the front entrance and then eyed me.

"Is that your bike?" he asked.

"Yes, it is."

"Ha," he frowned, then shook his head and continued with a note of sarcasm in his voice. "So where is your man?"

"Excuse me?" I asked carefully, not sure what he was implying.

"Where is your man? As a woman you cannot be traveling alone, especially not on a bike."

"Why not?

"It's too dangerous. What if something happens? A woman needs a man to protect her?"

Wordless, I shrugged my shoulders, took the room key and drove my bike around the building to the parking lot. I unloaded the bike, carried my heavy bags to the hotel room and went out for dinner.

Later I showered and then sat cross-legged on the bed, writing notes in my journal. I had ridden 541 miles on the 9th day of my journey. Exhausted, but still edgy, I felt the need to walk a labyrinth, just to relax before a good night sleep. With no sacred circles nearby, I opted to meditate. I straightened my spine, closed my eyes, and with a few deep breaths I relaxed my body, letting go of tension and muscle tightness. Then I drifted to a timeless state of deep tranquility and when I opened my eyes 45 minutes had passed.

Observing my reflection in the mirror, I noticed that my high cheekbones, blue almond shaped eyes and the arch of my brows reminded me of my father. My brother, Jörg, and I look alike, and we both look like our dad.

Thinking of my father, I realized that I knew only a fraction of who he had been. He was 37 when I was born and had already lived a full life. I remember him as a handsome man, tall, with broad shoulders, piercing green eyes, dark black hair and a full beard. He commanded attention when he entered a room and women turned their heads, touched by his charisma. People, who met him for the first time, guessed he was a doctor or a professor of some sort. But no, he was a farmer. Looking closer one saw the hardened callused hands. And over the years the heavy labor had stiffened his back.

In my father's mind, the most lasting words of wisdom had come from a respected town elder and commander of the Hitler Youth, who taught the boys to build trenches. From 1936 onward, being in the Hitler Youth was mandatory for every young German male. The elder said, "Karl, remember my words: Life is a struggle. You will see when you grow up."

He didn't have to wait long; life turned into hell and the war stole his youth. Then a bomb exploded on the front lawn of his parents' farm, killing everyone, except my dad, who ran as fast as he could when the shrapnel pierced his flesh.

My father had often quoted the town elder when I was growing up. Filled with the naïveté of my own youth, I assumed that the war had branded my dad with the fear of death and the belief that life had no purpose, only struggle and survival. But then what did I know?

The bomb blast had left a ringing in my dad's ear, a constant reminder of the fragility of life. He cared for his family and his farm, had a passion for horses and enjoyed being the best ballroom dancer in town. He loved to dance.

I fell asleep, my head filled with thoughts of my father.

The next day brought strong side winds. I left Elko, Nevada, early in the morning and my bike was plowing against the relentless forces advancing at eighty miles per hour. A couple of hundred miles on the open plains and the struggle against the wind emptied my mind of all clutter. I listened to the high-pitched whirl of air inside my helmet and the galloping beat of my machine, now recuperated after the Salt Lake Desert blaze. My body surrendered to the gusts, leaned over the tank, became streamlined.

Close to Reno, traffic intensified. Leaving the enchanting aura of endless spaces behind, I fueled up and then continued on I-80 into California. Fragments of Lake Tahoe's sapphire blue water peaked out behind emerald mountains to my left. Anticipating a joyous descent from the Sierras into the Bay Area, I looked forward to rolling through long curves surrounded by breathtaking vistas, one of the great joys of motorcycle riding.

Yellow signs announced construction areas and traffic channeled into one lane. Shocked, I saw the horrendous road conditions. Two inch deep tire tracks split the rough and uneven asphalt, a nightmare for any motorcyclist. Afraid of losing my balance, I steered carefully over the deep ridges. Grey concrete barriers divided the road. Paving crews of men wearing hard hats and orange vests operated heavy machinery. Numbed by the deafening noise, I inhaled the stench of hot asphalt. Then traffic began to crisscross from lane to lane, passing from one construction site to the next, each time forcing me across the tire tracks. My heart sank. The tough descent on impossible roads required utmost attention. By the time I reached Sacramento, rush hour traffic was heavy. I had planned to stay in Sacramento, but with only a hundred miles left to the Bay Area, I felt edgy and wanted to keep going. I phoned the Sisters of Mercy, where I had reservations for the next day. Yes, there was a room available tonight. Happy to hear the good news, I continued.

California surprised me with an appealing phenomenon: lane-splitting. Motorcyclists ride in between slow moving lanes of cars. I lane-splitted in Israel, but it is illegal in Pennsylvania, so I gave up the habit. Motorcycles began to pass me by the dozens, and I pulled in behind them, much better than standing in the heat inhaling exhaust fumes of the truck in front. Drivers were alert and courteously moved aside for the passing bikers. 'This is great,' I thought.

Twenty lanes opened approaching the Oakland Bay Bridge. I had never seen anything like it and steered to the middle. The lady at the toll booth mentioned a free passage for motorcycles in the outer left lanes. "Didn't know that," I said as she collected a dollar. Traffic channeled back into five lanes and vehicles crawled side by side toward the city, hovering high above the water. Getting tired, I was looking forward to reaching that day's final destination, when suddenly the view opened to downtown San Francisco and Alcatraz to my right. My heart beat faster and all fatigue vanished, replaced by an overwhelming sense of accomplishment. I had arrived at the West Coast. Surrounded by postcard views that I had seen so many times, I watched the fog roll in from the ocean and chase over hillside neighborhoods. I was in awe.

18

Half an hour later I left the congested traffic behind and pulled into the sanctuary of the Sisters of Mercy in Burlingame. I parked the bike in front of a white-tinted elegant three-story building, the mother house. The office manager and a friendly nun in her seventies welcomed me, rushing me to the dining room. Dinner was served only until 7:00 p.m. I had 15 minutes. "You must be hungry, having been out in the wind all day," the nun said. After a quick meal I unloaded the bike and settled into a sparse room, my home for the next three nights.

Thirsty for spiritual energy, I then followed the walking trail to the sacred circle. Surrounded by flower gardens and California oaks, the 11-circuit labyrinth felt tranquil and serene. I sat on a bench to relax and mentally prepare myself for the walk. I had reached the outer frontier of the West Coast, a baffling feat for the first settlers, who had arrived in horse-drawn wagons, but easy enough to accomplish in the 21st century. The true frontier is the mind, my beliefs and perceptions that shape my reality. In Eastern philosophy, the physical-material realm is called illusionary, a dream. 'What is really real?' I asked myself.

Created on sacred ground, the labyrinth carried the weight of history. The Native American Ohlone tribe had inhabited the San Francisco peninsula. Several oak trees on the Mercy Center property are 500 years old, and one could only wonder about the changes and evolution these trees had witnessed.

Father Thomas Hand, a Jesuit priest who lived in Japan for twenty-nine years and was a student of Zen, had built this labyrinth together with his meditation group after having received a generous donation. They carved the site out of a hill, laboring physically, shoveling tons of earth by hand, and not allowing modern equipment to disturb the peace. The labyrinth was laid out on stomped sand. The path's brick dividers lay embedded in the surface and appealing smooth river rocks marked the turns. The five-foot tall center stone, a monolith indigenous to the Bay Area, looked like a beacon connecting heaven and earth. Purple and white flowers surrounded the outer circle. A pine tree branched over the labyrinth, providing shade, guarding the seeker from being burned by the sun.

A grey-haired woman in a green dress, her life beautifully engraved into her skin, sat down next to me silently. After a while she looked over and said, "This is a holy place."

"Yes, I feel it," I responded.

"It is your first time here," she said, not inquiring, but simply stating a truth.

I nodded and then gave a summary of my road trip.

"Interesting." she said.

We sat side by side in silence. Then she stood up, said "Blessings on your journey," and walked away. Her soft-spoken words signaled the perfect time to embark into the labyrinth. The walk was easy; one step after the other I moved deeper into the labyrinth's force field. My body tingled, adjusting to the high vibration of energy. After the walk I returned to the guesthouse, took a shower and went to bed early, exhausted from 541 tough miles on the road.

The next morning I crawled out of bed still tired. Getting dressed, I noticed an open wound on the front of my left ankle. A flap of skin, the size of a quarter, revealed raw flesh, covered by a thin layer of fluid and blood. Mystified I sat back on the bed and examined the wound. No recollection surfaced about what could have happened. I covered the injury with a band aid and went to the dining room for breakfast. Deserted the evening before, the space was busy and people filled all the tables. I discovered one free chair, asked for permission to sit down and found myself in a circle of women from Alaska and Holland, attending a one-week meditation retreat. They praised a labyrinth in Juneau, located at the Shrine of St. Therese next to the bay, where one could hear whales sing. I took note of the location for a future journey.

Awakened by plenty of coffee, cereal and eggs, I proceeded to the labyrinth and sat on the bench overlooking the magnificent sacred circle. A gentle morning light touched the monolith, casting mesmerizing shades, transforming the rock into a long-bearded monk covered by a flowing robe.

I focused on my breathing and was still wondering how I got the cut. Then an insight came. I had fallen out of bed, and the rough carpet scratched my ankle's skin. Aware that at night we leave our physical bodies and travel to the upper worlds, I asked myself which demons I had encountered during my dreams. Or did my tired muscles simply cramp, throwing me out of bed, a result from sitting on my bike for more than a thousand miles the last two days? No clear answer emerged. It could have been both.

I feel that my duty as a seeker is to gain understanding about the forces that operate on me. The physical realm and my life experience represent a mere reflection of something greater. Driven to keep asking, I yearn to connect the dots.

Having reached the West Coast and a new frontier, I sensed that the moment had arrived to walk a timeline and review my life. It is said that a life not reflected upon is a life not worth living, but merely existence. Looking at the labyrinth, I wondered if there is any better way to reveal the flow of time than in a circle. Time, usually perceived in a linear way, makes more sense when examined in a non-linear round way. The point located in the center of the circle is the constant measure; the beginning and the end.

Barefoot I walked over to the labyrinth's entrance; taking the first step I let my mind wander back to my youth. I recalled the constant quarrels with my father, the discrepancy between the life I wanted to live and the life I was supposed to live. I had surrendered to my family's wishes and dreamed about riding bikes, traveling and becoming a painter, which was inconceivable to my parents. They were practical, down-to-earth dairy farmers in the Lower Rhine Valley of Germany and envisioned that I would learn a solid profession, which would assure a secure future. My search was for freedom and adventure, not for security. Of course, I was young. My parents pointed out that whatever I was seeking, it was not real. The 'real' reality was filled with structure, responsibility and struggle. They called me a dreamer.

I turned and turned deeper into the labyrinth. When I looked up to the foggy California morning sky an image emerged. It felt as if my younger self walked right next to me. I looked different then, at twenty-one. My hair was one-inch short and colored bright henna red. I wore rainbow-colored pants, which I had bought at Third World store, and my shirt was painted with abstract designs, one of my own creations. In these days, I was painting shirts, hoping that one day I would sell them at markets. I also saw myself wearing comfortable Birkenstock sandals and socks. I burst out laughing. Back then, before traveling the world, I didn't know that Germans always stood out wearing sandals and socks, a terrible fashion mistake in any other country.

At that time in my life I was ready to break free. I had sincerely tried to be the obedient daughter, tried to follow my parents' wishes, and had dabbled in different impossible career choices: two months of secretarial school, one year of agriculture training on a farm, two semesters of agriculture studies at the university in Bonn, ten months of studies in the hotel industry. I was suffocating. With growing urgency, I knew there was a life to be lived and there was no more time to be wasted.

19

I yearned to explore and figure out what to do with the rest of my life. I saw my younger self researching books about South America and Israel. I had debated whether to go backpacking or to volunteer on a Kibbutz in Israel. These communal settlements offered free lodging for an exchange of six to eight hours of farm work per day. But my youth on a dairy farm had provided me with plenty of opportunities for labor. Growing up, I cleaned stables, milked cows, fed the animals and packed hay and straw on wagons at harvest time. Volunteering on a Kibbutz meant a pre-set daily structure. Not wanting structure or responsibility, I planned to flow freely and see where life would take me.

I took the next step deeper into the labyrinth and felt a shift. My body was overcome with a sense of lightness, and then flashes of insight streamed at a fast pace into my consciousness revealing bits and pieces of my past. I was twenty-one, had booked a ticket to Rio de Janeiro and took off on a ten-week solo backpacking trip through Brazil.

I watched images of my younger self boarding a Royal Air Maroc flight from Amsterdam to Rio de Janeiro via Casablanca. The date was December 31, 1987. It was my first transatlantic crossing. I made new friends during the flight and toasted with champagne for three New Year's festivities, according to the time zones of Holland, Morocco and Brazil.

Leaves rustled in an oak tree next to the labyrinth. The noise startled me. I looked up and saw a small blue bird spreading its wings taking off into flight. I smiled. 'Nice metaphor,' I thought. I spread my wings when I took off to Brazil.

Then my memories took me onward, ten days into the Brazil trip, to the Foz de Iguaçu Falls, the world's largest waterfalls at the border between Brazil, Argentina and Paraguay. I watched myself exploring the walkways around the falls and taking a break on an observation deck, crowded with people. Thousands of gallons of water poured off the cliff above. The thundering force gushed by. Exhausted from the tropical heat, I sat on the floor and watched the cascading water, surrounded by the lush green vegetation of the rainforest. I took a package of Drum tobacco out of my bag and rolled a cigarette.

The young man to my left looked surprised. "You're from Holland?" he asked, pointing to the Dutch tobacco.

"Germany," I answered. "Would you like some?" I passed him the tobacco.

"I am Ronen," he said while rolling a cigarette. "I used to live in Amsterdam."

"Nice to meet you. I am Dorit."

"Dorit? Are you Jewish?" he asked.

"No."

"Well, you know, Dorit is a common Israeli name."

"Israeli?" Surprised, my mind wandered to the countless times people had asked if my name wasn't Doris or Dorothee.

"Are you Israeli?" I inquired.

"Yes. I am traveling with my friends. We served in the Israeli Defense Force, and now we are backpacking for a year in South America."

"You are traveling a whole year?" Impressed, I studied his face, his dark brown eyes, black curls, falling over his eyebrows.

"There is a lot to see," he smiled.

Ronen, his Israeli friends and I traveled together for the next days and then took the train from Curitiba to Paranagua, a 62-mile scenic voyage, which winds its way through the Serra do Mar Mountains to the coast. A month later we would meet again in Olinda to celebrate the carnival.

Looking back on this encounter nearly twenty years later, I realized that meeting the Israelis was the key moment that eventually would lead me to Israel.

But my mind didn't linger with this moment. I kept walking at a slow pace deeper into the Burlingame labyrinth. I focused on revisiting places in my life that had formed and shaped me into who I had become. My consciousness catapulted me onward to the next important moment during my backpacking trip in Brazil. It jumped to Sao Paulo, Brasilia, then to Manaus and focused on the ferry that I took down the Amazon River to Belem. I saw myself swinging in a hammock, watching the scenery glide by as the ferry meandered the river turns. Lush green jungle closed in. My hands nearly touched the foliage. Hammocks had been a requirement for the four day journey. There were no cabins or beds. Tourists settled on the upper deck in an open compartment, hanging three hammocks on top of each other. A dozen Israelis, some Europeans, two Americans and Toni from South Africa had been my fellow boat mates. The locals traveled in the lower compartment, together with their small animals, goats, chickens and young pigs.

During the Amazon passage, I became friends with Toni and two Israelis, Joe and Shlomo. Heading for the same destination, we decided to travel together. One night we stayed in Belem, the port city of the Amazon Delta. The next morning we embarked on a twenty-four hour bus journey to Fortaleza, and then continued on the back of a truck to Canoa Cebrada, a village with no electricity nor indoor plumbing built in the dunes east of Fortaleza. Exhausted and tired we arrived at dark, rented a hut, and set up for the night in our sleeping bags. The men dozed off immediately.

Sweaty and overheated, I decided to go for a quick ocean swim to wash off the dust from the road. Swiftly I left the village and followed the salty scent of the sea. Wind caressed my short hair and the sound of gushing ocean waves called me. My eyes quickly adjusted to the dark, admiring a slim slice of moon in the sky and the bright-shining stars. I walked down the dunes to the sea. My toes touched the water, a refreshing rush sparked inside my body. I took off my clothes and ran naked into the water. My skin cooled while floating on my back to the rhythm of the waves. The beach disappeared farther in the distance. Every once in a while I touched the ground below with one foot. The water was shallow, and I felt safe.

Entering a timeless state, carried by the ocean, I was weightless and free. My ears dipped below the surface. The deep bubbly sound of the waves sounded like the inside of a mother's womb.

Suddenly the water changed. I turned on my belly and the beach was gone. My foot reached into the depth, unable to touch the ground. An undercurrent took me out to the ocean. Using all my strength I swam against the current. Fighting the waves I struggled and failed. I envisioned my parents in mourning. My dad was holding my mom, both sobbing, their eyes reddened from tears. What if I could not get out of this? What if I would die now? What if my body was never found? Horrified I heard my mother's plea before I went on this trip.

"Don't go by yourself; it is too dangerous."

I swam as hard as I could. Sharp pain burned my muscles. Salty water filled my throat as I choked. Not giving up, I felt my heart race and rage against my ribcage. Panicky shivers erupted within me. There was no use in screaming. Nobody would hear me. Focusing my thoughts on living, I forced away the desperate image of my distressed parents. The words 'I live, I live, I am alive' spun inside my head. I fought, and I escaped the current and my sure death.

My legs trembled as I waded through the shallow water and then threw myself onto the beach. I sucked the air in deeply. I felt the weight of my body press against the sand. A cool breeze brushed over my skin. Goose bumps tingled all over as I looked up to the sky. Millions of stars illumined the night. Shaken by my own mortality I fell apart and cried.

Far removed from this moment in my past, I realized its still strong grip on me. I took deep breaths and felt as if I couldn't get enough air into my lungs. I took several steps forward, deeper into the labyrinth. I counted aloud from one to twelve to calm myself. Then I continued to walk in silence and refocused my mind on the days that I had stayed in Canoa Cebrada following my ocean swim. Even though I was traumatized by the near drowning experience, life went on. Drenched with sunlight, the beach and the ocean seemed like innocent friends inviting me to relax and replenish.

Then suddenly my mind jerked me back from sunny Brazilian beaches to the German cold colorless winter. It was March 1988, shortly after my ten-week trip. I was sitting in the kitchen of our farm overlooking the grey, wet, foggy landscape, so typical of the Lower Rhine Valley. I had just returned from Brazil and already felt I was suffocating. My parents sat across from me, demanding answers. In their mind I had completed my wildest dream, and it was time to settle down and come up with a clear plan for the future.

My head though was filled with anticipation for more adventures. I told them about the people I had met, the places I had seen. Of course I made sure to never mention my near drowning experience.

They weren't impressed.

"I had to travel to Brazil to find out the origin of my name," I said. "Dorit is a Hebrew name. And you know how often I asked you about the origin of my name when I was growing up."

"Yes, I know," my mom said. "I have no idea what got into me to call you Dorit. But what does that have to do with anything?" Her voice was shrill.

"To me that means everything," I said. "Maybe I have to go to Israel to find out?"

"You need to get your feet on the ground." My mom's face turned red. "See what real life looks like: work hard, raise a family, and be responsible..."

"That cannot be it; career, husband, children, a nice house," I interrupted her. "There has to be more to life. I just got started. I met all these backpackers who are traveling for a whole year. Two and a half months is nothing. I can imagine going on a longer trip next time."

"Enough." My dad slammed his fist on the table. "I don't want to hear any of it. When are you coming to your senses?"

My mom nodded in agreement. "All your crazy escapades. No other parent would allow that. Look at everyone you went to school with; all of them are building nice careers and nice lives. And what are you doing? It's unacceptable. I don't want to be ashamed of my own daughter."

This went on and on. For me there was no way back. I was happy with my life exactly the way it was. I wanted adventure, uncertainty and infinite possibilities. My brush with death in Cano Cebrada had taught me that life could end too quickly. There was no time to be wasted. From my point of view, I was done arguing with my parents. I wouldn't listen to them.

I moved into an apartment with friends, found a temporary job at a factory, saved money and researched where I would go. Israel was on top of my list of desirable places. And with my new connections to the Israeli friends with whom I had traveled in Brazil, it would be an easy transition. Tel Aviv emerged as my next destination.

20

Reveling in memories, I had lost awareness of the environment. Chatting voices returned me to that present moment at the Sisters of Mercy in Burlingame. Two women walked by, and I wondered if they intended to join the journey into the labyrinth. They never looked over or saw me and continued to the meditation garden. I refocused my thoughts on the timeline, to revisit moments essential for my evolution and jumped instantly to the period when my life had changed dramatically.

It was March 1989. I couldn't wait to leave Germany; the world was big and life was filled with possibilities. I arrived in Israel and immediately enrolled at the language school Ulpan Meir on King George Street in the bustling center of Tel Aviv. I was excited to study Hebrew. The school was an international melting pot. The 30 students in my class had come from Holland, Britain, France, Russia, United States, Brazil, Argentina, the Philippines, Germany and Iran. I was studying six days a week for six hours a day. My head buzzed with new words and grammar.

After completing the half-year language program, I was accepted to the Avni Institute for Fine Arts in Tel Aviv - Jaffo. I yearned to study art, and being far away from home, I had finally escaped my parents' sphere of influence. I was determined to live my dream. I studied figurative painting, landscapes and nudes, and was intrigued with abstract art. The works of the Israeli artists Lea Nikel and Moshe Gershuni impressed me deeply. Rough edged chunks of colors filled Nikel's canvases, overlaid by calligraphic scribbles. Gershuni's works included mysterious dark surfaces, burning with fire. The occasional symbols of the cross or the Star of David spoke directly to the viewer's soul. The German artist Joseph Beuys was my favorite. Beuys was not only an artist but also a shaman. He created art with a variety of materials; the most eccentric were felt and fat. Discovering the healing power of art, he had boldly stated, "Every human being is an artist."

His incredible ability to command a sheet of paper with a single line of pencil mesmerized me. One fragile line emanated immeasurable strength, as if containing all secrets of the universe.

But I felt frustrated. None of my attempts to create abstract art had succeeded. Unable to step beyond copying what my eyes saw, I was bound to models and landscapes. My effort to translate my inner world of feelings and images into paintings had failed. The door stayed locked and I did not have the key to open it.

At that same time I began to practice yoga and became interested in the healing arts. One evening Ronit, a friend at Yoga School, and I sat together drinking tea.

"Dorit, I started studying with an incredible bio-energetic healer," she said. "I remember that you had mentioned you are interested in learning more about healing. His new course starts soon. You might like it."

"What's his name?" I asked.

"Rafi Rosen."

"Oh, yes. I have heard of him. People seem to be very impressed with his work."

"Impressed is an understatement. He saved my mother's life," Ronit said. "My mom was suffering from frequent back pain for some time. She saw a doctor who prescribed pain medication. But it didn't help much, so she decided to try the unconventional route. She asked me to accompany her to an appointment with the healer." Ronit was of a gentle and quiet nature, her body slender, and her brown eyes set back, which emphasized her strong eyebrows. She never talked much, but I could see how excited she got telling the story. In a fluid motion she swung her long black hair over her shoulders. She beamed. "Rafi moved his hand twenty inches above my mother's spine and concluded that she had to see a doctor immediately. A tumor needed to be removed. He diagnosed her within two minutes. Then he asked her to lie down on a treatment bed and gave her a half hour healing session. He never touched her; only once he put his hands on the area where he said the tumor was located. When we left my mom's pain was gone. She went on to see a different doctor and tests revealed a small malignant tumor. Her surgery was scheduled without delay. Had she not seen Rafi she might not have found out until it would have been too late."

"And he teaches how to do that?" I was curious.

"Yes," Ronit said. "The course is life changing."

The next day I signed up for the training. The classes took place at Rafi's home on Balfour Street in Tel Aviv. Our group of 20 students sat in a circle on soft comfortable mats. A fresh breeze streamed through the open windows. The green scent of trees filled the air. Rafi's intense blue eyes moved quickly. His grey curls reached his shoulders. He introduced the subject.

"You are much more than a physical body. You are surrounded by fields of energetic consciousness and you will learn to sense these fields. The energetic information transcends time and space and influences all aspects of your lives: your health, your thinking, and your ability to relate to people."

Rafi instructed us to pair up and to move the palm of one hand over the top of the other person's head. Closing our eyes we focused on the kinesthetic perception. Moving my right hand above my partner's head, at first I felt nothing. I focused on abdominal breathing and tried to slow the chatter in my mind. Slowly I sensed a prickling sensation. A gentle stream of heat emanated from the top of my partner's head. Moving my hand aside to her shoulder the sensation ceased. For comparison, I used my left hand and noticed a different sensation; the energy felt like a fresh mountain stream. Rafi explained the different sensations with the fact that as one hand gives, the other receives. My ability to perceive energies intensified the more I relaxed. Astounded to sense something that my eyes didn't see, I practiced the exercises daily.

Throughout the following weeks I refined my abilities to distinguish subtle energies and detected the congested clutter typical for a headache or the deep dark hum indicating a clogged artery in a patient's heart. Thrilled I learned the principles of energetic healing.

My concept of reality shifted; my mind opened. Entering a process of redefining who I would be as a human being, I began to see life in a new way. One day the class focused on giving up control. Rafi explained, "Being in control all the time messes up your lives. You get stuck, your energy field gets stuck and then you get ill. It is futile to think that you are in control. Only when you learn to let go can you truly enjoy the flow of life."

Rafi stood up, brushed the curls out of his face and clapped his hands. "Let's all get up and form a circle. Today we'll practice an exercise that will allow you to let go of control. One at a time you will lie down in the center. You will shake your head and pound your arms and legs into the mats as fast as you can until your mind starts spinning. Go far beyond your comfort zone; keep going for as long as you can and then relax. The rest of us will encourage you, and once you have lost complete control, we'll focus on sending healing energies."

My turn came. My body sank into the comfortable mats; I inhaled deeply and then slowly shook my head, my arms and legs. I looked up into the cheering faces of the fellow students, then closed my eyes and increased the speed. My head started spinning. Dizzy, I tried to resist but couldn't stop the surge. An untamed force of madness burst through me. With no thoughts and nothing to hold onto, I went faster and faster until I couldn't sense my body. It felt as if a wild outrage ripped open every one of my cells. I heard myself screaming, and then it stopped.

I surrendered, out of breath, lungs pumping. My closed eyes witnessed a brilliant white golden light all around. I was peaceful, yet alert, awakened and energized in a way I had never known before. The cells of my body pulsated with new life energy. Slowly opening my eyes, I saw light all around. And then the picture emerged of the smiling, loving faces of my classmates. Their hands directed toward me, I observed the brilliant light streaming from their palms. Extending my gaze I viewed the fields of light surrounding everyone with dazzling intensity. I rubbed my eyes in disbelief, but the light shone bright and brilliant.

My broadened perception lasted until the end of the healing session. Later that afternoon I went to art school. My easel stood positioned next to the ceiling-high windows. Bright daylight streamed into the classroom. Enjoying the view of the Mediterranean Sea, I saw Tel Aviv's high-rise buildings in the distance. Looking at my empty canvas, I prepared to paint another vase of flowers working out in detail the intricate play of light and color. As soon as I picked up the brush, I knew something felt different. I trusted my instinct, remembered Rafi's words that we have to get out of our own way, give up control and let life flow. Intuitively, I began throwing quick brush strokes of thick oil paint on the canvas. It all happened so quickly; I had no time to question what I was doing. A rhythmic dance of determined movement amazed me, revealing colorful results on the canvas. Creating abstract art felt easy.

Something opened up in me. The unknown that I had not been able to grasp suddenly made perfect sense. I entered a new dimension of awareness. My studies in the field of energy healing had affected the way I was doing art and thus had changed the way I perceived reality. Like a stone of creativity thrown into a pond, it had inspired many beautiful ripples growing and expanding in all directions.

I stopped, took a deep breath and stood straight in the Sisters of Mercy Labyrinth. Then I stretched my arms and lifted my open palms toward the still foggy sky. Looking back I was amazed at how quickly everything had fallen into place for me in Israel. Within the first two years I had completed language school, was studying art at the most renowned art institute in Tel Aviv and explored uncharted territory by learning bio-energetic healing. I knew what came next, felt a wave of excitement, stepped onward in my life review and deeper into the labyrinth.

Instantly I was catapulted to my art studio in Tel Aviv. I saw my younger self sitting on the floor, rolling a cigarette with Drum tobacco, drinking strong black coffee and examining large canvases. I looked different then, very thin, my face chiseled, my hair longer and pulled back into a ponytail. My standard outfit of jeans and white T-shirt was smeared with oil colors. I had just completed a series of oil paintings called 'Seeking Blue.' The series had been inspired by a dream about a true story that my dad had told me. Shortly before I was born a white whale lost its way and swam up the River Rhine, past our farm, three hundred miles to Cologne until it turned around and found its way back to the North Sea.

In the dream, which later inspired the paintings, I saw myself in my hometown, Rees, standing on a lookout on top of the fortified city walls. The fertile land stretched out flat like a sheet, cut apart by the leisurely flowing river. Everything familiar seemed completely new. The entire world glowed with blue, different shades and variations of luminous blue light. Even the solid objects, like houses and trees, were illumined by an internal glimmer of blue, making them appear non-material. The whale swam upstream; gracefully he radiated wisdom and strength. I felt overwhelmed by the presence of the gigantic animal. For several moments he looked into my eyes and seemed to communicate. I was seeking to understand, but could I? His world was beyond my world. The whale continued on its journey and I marveled at the incredible blue colors of the landscape, the River Rhine and the wide open sky. Just then I sensed that only the whale was real.

I had tried to recapture the luminous blue light, the sense of flow, the deep blue water. I splashed abundant strokes of blue oil paint on the canvas, followed by thin and deliberate layers of aquamarine, azure, cerulean and hints of turquoise. The paintings evolved over a half-year period. Each new layer of paint required sufficient time to dry. I spent hours sitting in front of the paintings, looking at them and taking them in. With a patient eye I considered my next step. What would be important to accentuate with a fresh layer of paint? When I finally picked up the brush, new revelations surfaced. The results never obeyed my planning, always a million times better than anything I could have imagined.

I was happy with the paintings, happy with my life. Then I saw myself checking the clock and realizing that I was late. I jumped up, locked the studio and raced on my bicycle across Tel Aviv to the motorcycle driving school.

Next I saw myself taking driving lessons. My dream of riding a motorcycle was finally coming true and I had the biggest smile on my lips.

I stopped again in my tracks; the images of my life review cheered me up. I laughed out loud, smiled and took another step into the labyrinth. Quick flashes played the next important life events in front of my mind's eye.

A few days after I had passed my test and got my motorcycle license, I received a phone call. A lawyer had redecorated his office space and was shopping for modern art. He asked to visit my studio.

He came the next day and without hesitation picked two oil paintings from the series 'Seeking Blue.' I couldn't believe my luck when he wrote the check. My art sold. I felt overjoyed. With the nice sum of money that had miraculously entered my life, I was able to afford my first motorcycle: a bright red Czechoslovakian Jawa 350.

21

The memories of my first motorcycle brought pure joy. I felt like dancing and leaped into the air. Then I took a few deep breaths, tried to contain myself, but couldn't stop smiling. I felt grateful for the blissful moments the life review allowed me to relive, and then I journeyed deeper into the labyrinth.

The Jawa's maximum speed reached 75 miles per hour. Bulky and sturdy, the bike's ancient technology featured a two-stroke engine, and I had to mix oil in with the fuel. During the hot Mediterranean summer, I rode in short pants, a T-shirt and sandals. The law in Israel required wearing a helmet, my only safety measure until one day in late August.

Working on a series of paintings called 'The Passion of Life,' I glued burned books and Israeli soil onto big canvases. The rough structures overflowed with bold layers of oil color. I had tried to convey my inner conflict of being a German living among Jewish people and covered my paintings with endless black tears, yellow Stars of David, and violent flames of destruction.

The tube of cadmium yellow released its last squeeze of oil paint, and I made a quick run to Arik's Art Supplies. We had endured five dry months without a single drop of rain. This morning, though, stunning dark blue clouds covered the sky and emptied their refreshing mass of water onto the thirsty earth. The rain brought a blissful freshness to the city, washing away the dust and making breathing an invigorating pleasure. At the same time, the first rain transformed the streets into treacherous hazards. The oil and dirt, sealed into the asphalt's surface during the summer, emerged dangerously.

I jumped on the Jawa and kicked the starter with a few strong pushes of my right foot. The engine came to life howling. I opened the throttle, rushing through the congested streets of the city. The art store came into sight, easels and canvas on display and special offers written in bold red letters on the windows. Just one last turn and I would be there. Suddenly I floated weightless for a moment as my bike slipped from underneath me. I tumbled to the asphalt. My bare skin ripped open as it slid across the black tar. I moaned in pain. Cars stopped immediately and pedestrians hurried and helped me get up. I walked away with a few bruises and an agonizing road rash, a layer of sensitive skin scraped of my arms and legs. The next day, I got a leather jacket and started wearing jeans and shoes when I rode.

The bike, my only vehicle, had served a multitude of purposes, including weekly grocery shopping. Tel Aviv's Karmel Market stretched over half a mile and meandered through a maze of side streets. Busy merchants praised their goods, abundant piles of fresh fruit and vegetables, and competed for every customer. Fresh oranges and grapefruit cut into halves saturated the air with a stimulating crisp scent. The brightest colors of red, orange, yellow and green created an elaborate feast for the eye.

I loved the herb stand. Bundles of fresh parsley, mint, basil and sage sold for one Shekel. Loading the groceries on the bike's handle bars, I balanced the heavy plastic bags, driving home carefully.

I also transported my canvases on the bike. A friend would come along for the ride, sit on the back and hold a canvas, a delicate balancing act. In such a manner, we carried one canvas at a time.

Riding a motorcycle rewarded me with the freedom to leave the big city on Sabbath. Public transportation shut down completely on the day God rested. I was independent to travel north to the Sea of Galilee, my favorite destination, or explore secluded beaches. My friend Karin often joined the excursions. Later she rescued a tiny kitten, barely fit to survive, and refused to leave her at home. The baby cat joined our adventures, a third passenger, safely tucked into Karin's backpack.

Remembering the biker kitten, I chuckled and then was surprised to have reached the labyrinth's center. I returned back to the present moment and focused on the labyrinth in Burlingame, California. Grateful for the multitude of life experiences, I circled the monolith three times. Events seemed connected, governed by a higher force, revealing themselves in a purposeful way, even though sometimes one could experience life as walking blindfolded and tapping in the dark. Walking the labyrinth and contemplating a life review allowed me to see the journey's meaningful unfolding. The rough sand tingled underneath my bare feet. The sky, foggy until now, ripped open revealing its infinite blue and warm rays of rising sun. I molded my open palms around the monolith, gliding along the jagged and smooth surface; still cold from the night, it felt strong and solid. A bird sang and red and violet flowers turned their heads toward the sun.

I began to retrace my steps out of the labyrinth. I concentrated my intention on staying in the moment. I had seen different times of my past, re-lived them and felt full and saturated without the need to remember more. There would be other days to recall the puzzle pieces of my life and to reflect on how I got to where I was.

But in the labyrinth I was not in control. My mind jumped to the spring of 1993. I surrendered and reconnected to the moment when I had attended a lecture about holistic medicine and reflexology at the Mahut School for Complementary Medicine and Holism, located in the business district in South Tel Aviv. A fellow student at Rafi Rosen's had praised the reflexology training. Mahut in Hebrew means 'essence of being.' The school's founders were Kabbalists, and the spiritual understanding of the world was an integrated part of the curriculum. I had been curious to learn how through the feet the entire body could be healed.

I entered the classroom. The busy chatter of two dozen people filled the space with life. Tall windows in the back of the room opened to a neighboring building. A cool evening breeze streamed in. I felt at ease and recognized familiar faces.

The teacher, a handsome man, blond hair, a charismatic smile and friendly blue eyes, entered the room. Everyone turned silent in his calm and peaceful presence. He introduced himself as Gilad Shadmon and then asked, "What is reality?"

He looked at every one of us, taking in our response. The question surprised me. Reality seemed simple, obvious and easy to describe. But as I reflected upon it, I didn't find words.

"Well, we are gathered here to listen to your lecture and that is our reality," a woman in her mid-forties said.

"So would you say that we all experience the same reality?" Gilad asked.

"Yes, absolutely," she agreed.

"Hm, my reality as the presenter is different than yours, and then every one of you has a different experience, too. Let's examine if there is an objective reality." Gilad moved toward the blackboard reaching for the chalk. He drew a box and five openings.

"This is the individual human being," he explained. "Every one of us lives in our own separate box and perceives the world through the five senses and our unique set of beliefs and judgments. All function as a limiting filter. Our filter only allows us to see outside of ourselves, what exists within us, from the view inside our box. In psychological terms this is called projection."

Gilad painted more boxes on the board. "So we exist inside these separate boxes, disconnected by our limiting ideas. Therefore we can conclude that in our mundane world there is no objective reality."

I raised my hand: "So if every one of us experiences a different reality, is it possible to change our realities?" I was intrigued. In my mind, my father's voice said loud and clear, "Your dreams aren't real. The one true reality is not what you think it is. There is no place for your lofty ideas. True reality is filled with hardship, labor and difficulty."

"That is a very important question. Yes, you can change your reality," Gilad said, "You begin by asking the right questions."

"What are the right questions?"

Gilad looked straight into my eyes, "Did you ever ask yourself, Who am I? Where do I come from? What is the purpose of life?"

"Many times."

"These are the right questions. Ask and when you are ready to listen, the answers will come. You will embark on a journey of awakening, and one day you will remember who you are."

Gilad drew a circle around the boxes and said, "When you ask the right questions, a new impulse is born and you yearn to break free from your limiting beliefs. As a matter of fact, we live in a field of ultimate truth, an

all encompassing light, which is always there, and it is up to the individual
to evolve toward this truth."

Gilad cleaned the board. "You see, perception of reality is a very complex
subject; we will study this in the holistic training." Then he looked at his
watch and said, "It is time to tell you about Reflexology." He drew the sole
of a foot and the image of a human body on the blackboard and went on to
describe the ancient Chinese healing art, whereby the entire body can be
treated through the feet.

Touched by what I felt was authentic truth; I knew studying with Gilad
would enable me to expand my consciousness. I signed up for the training
and studied at Mahut for the next years.

Then my awareness jumped back to the present moment in the
Burlingame labyrinth. The sun warmed my skin. I felt at ease. I took
another step and then my mind zoomed in quickly to the time when I had
learned an astonishing fact about my father. By then I was a year into my
studies at the Mahut School for Complementary Medicine and Holism.

One Sunday afternoon, the first workday of the week in Israel, the
phone rang. Running late for school, I was hurrying to put my holistic
medicine books into a backpack. I wondered if I should answer or just let
the machine get the call. But then I picked up and heard my mom's voice
trembling in outrage, "Your father is going insane."

"What?" I said.

"Your father is going insane."

"Mom, calm down. What happened?"

"Your brother's friend Klaus came over to introduce his new girlfriend
of four weeks. Now guess what your father did."

"Mom, I don't know. What did he do?"

"He took Klaus aside and congratulated him on having a bun in the oven."

"Seriously," I laughed. "Why would he do that?"

"I told you, he is going insane."

I paused and then asked, "Well, what does dad have to say about it?"

"I don't care. It's an embarrassment. Klaus is going to tell his family
what your father said, and soon the whole town will be talking about it."

"Okay, this doesn't make sense. Can I talk to my father?"

At the other end of the line was silence. My mom didn't say another word. I heard a door open and upset she yelled, "Karl, your daughter wants to speak with you."

A few moments later I listened to a muffled noise and assumed my mom had handed over the phone.

"Hi honey." My dad sounded calm and oblivious to the commotion he had caused.

"Dad, what's going on?"

"Klaus got his new girlfriend pregnant."

"And how would you know that?"

"I see it."

"You see it?" I laughed. "Dad, there is no belly after four weeks. What do you see?" I was ready to agree with my mom.

"The moment a woman conceives, the light around her face changes," he said.

"Are you serious? And you can see that?" I asked.

"Yes. Just nobody wants to hear about it."

"Dad, I never knew that about you."

"Dorit, you don't know everything. But your mom does. I saw the light around her when she was pregnant with you and your brother, but she doesn't want to hear any of it."

"Dad, that's unbelievable. When did you start seeing the light?"

"When I was five. I delivered eggs to the neighbor's house and saw a strange shimmering light around the woman's face. I knew immediately what it meant. I ran home and told my mother. She told me to shut up and never talk such nonsense again."

"And then?" I inquired.

"I watched the neighbor's wife and a few months later everyone saw that she was pregnant. I never mentioned another word to my mother but observed quietly. Over the years I learned that I perceive things that nobody else sees. But it's not of much use; it only got me into trouble."

"Why?" I asked.

"Because people don't want to know."

"Dad, this totally blows my mind. I'd love to talk to you, but I've got to go."

We said goodbye. I grabbed my backpack and rushed to school.

When I arrived, Gilad was just about to enter the classroom. Out of breath I asked, "Gilad, do you have one moment, please? I need to ask you something important." My teacher smiled patiently. "Sure."

"I just talked to my dad. He sees things. I never knew that about him. But he says the light around a woman's face changes when she is expecting, and he has been able to perceive it since his childhood."

"Well, that is not uncommon. So your dad sees energy fields." Gilad said.

"Hm, I don't really know. He just mentioned a light."

"You should ask him for details. Does he see colors? Your dad is a farmer; does he see it with cows?"

"I'll ask. It's just such a surprise. You taught me how to see energy fields. I would never have thought that my dad sees the invisible."

"That is the beauty of life. It's full of surprises." My teacher smiled.

Then we entered the classroom. I took a seat, and Gilad started the lesson by introducing new reflexology points to the class. I shifted my gaze and focused on the white wall behind him. Immediately his energy field became visible. I saw a brilliant sphere of light extending three feet beyond his physical body. His field was brightest when he taught; then a brilliant funnel extended more than five feet high above the crown of his head. During a normal conversation, the funnel shrank. I continued to focus on my classmates. Everyone's field looked different, depending on the intensity of their vibration and their emotions.

The next day I spoke with my father.

"Dad, can you see when animals get pregnant?" I asked.

"No, not animals."

"And do you see colors?"

"No, there is a new light around a woman's face the moment she conceives. That's all. Why do you ask?"

"During my training I learned to see energy fields that surround every living being, usually I see a white light, but sometimes also colors."

"Hm." My dad paused and then said, "Why would you want to learn that? What is it going to be useful for?" Then he changed the subject.

Two months later my brother called to confirm that my dad was right. Klaus' new girlfriend was expecting.

127

22

Step by step I followed the path farther away from the labyrinth's center. Different memories kept coming, and I noticed the gentle flow of emotions arising. I sensed my immense curiosity about life and felt joy and excitement. Images flashed in front of my inner eye. I saw myself riding my motorcycle and studying at the Mahut School for Complementary Medicine and Holism. The images passed quickly and took me to my first art opening in Tel Aviv, then Jerusalem and next to the artist village En Hod, near Haifa. I couldn't stay or linger; the inner pictures kept changing, once showing my younger self at the Yoga Studio, together with a room full of students, all of us standing on our heads, and then switching to the farm where I rode a horse three times a week. Next I saw myself working as a waitress and cleaning apartments. 'Oh yes,' I thought, 'this is how I financed it all.'

Then, as if to emphasize a point, the flow of inner pictures halted. I saw the restaurant at Hotel Yamit, right on the Mediterranean Sea in Tel Aviv. There was utter confusion when four of us six waitresses were called Dorit. Our manager had assigned us numbers to keep the orders apart.

Even now I remain baffled by the mystery of my Hebrew name. The images stopped and I took a deep breath. I was in awe about my life and wondered how I had managed to do it. But the moment I asked this question the energy in the labyrinth shifted suddenly and came down on me with a heavy weight. A blow hit my intestines, and I went onto my knees. I knew

I was alone in the labyrinth; nobody had seen me. More images surfaced and I wanted to throw up.

I was catapulted back to the classroom at Mahut. It was 1994, the day after a suicide bomber had exploded bus number five in the heart of Tel Aviv, just steps away from Dizengoff Circle.

At the time, Prime Minister Yitzhak Rabin was attempting to broker a peace deal with the Palestinians and the bus bombings were at their peak.

One chair was empty. Adi was missing and everyone kept silent; we knew what this could mean. Adi took bus number five every day. Then Gilad entered the classroom.

"Adi's husband called this afternoon; she is all right, just minor injuries. She was waiting at the bus stop. The bus exploded before it reached her." All of us sighed in relief.

A week later, Adi returned to school. Her tall and slender body was graceful as always; she was a professional dancer in a modern dance company. She carried her spine straight, her shoulders back. Every one of her movements seemed deliberate and thought through. A long-sleeved shirt covered the bandages. During the first break she told me what had happened. Her hazel brown eyes stared to the ground. "I was late for dance practice," she said. "I tried to get to the front of the line. There were a dozen people waiting. It was morning rush hour and the previous bus had already passed without stopping. It was filled to the last spot. Then I saw the next bus approaching. Every seat was taken. People stood in the aisles. I looked at the driver, hoped that he would stop, just to fit in a few more people.

Then the bus blew up right in front of my eyes. It was a horrendous noise. Balls of fire shot off into all directions." Adi paused.

I wanted to put my arm around her but hesitated. Adi's body was injured and bruised, and I was afraid to hurt her. She pressed both of her hands against her head, rubbing them against her short black hair and then went on to tell how the detonation wave tossed her up and then threw her onto the sidewalk, and she found her entire body covered with burn marks and pieces of smoldering human flesh of those killed. "The stench was the worst," she said.

In the following weeks, Adi often came late to class apologizing that she had gotten on the wrong bus or had exited at the wrong station. She was baffled by her own confusion.

"I have no idea how it happened," she said, shaking her head.

As time went by, Adi noticed that as a dancer she was able to reach new heights in her performance. "It is as if I am not connected to my body any more," she explained. "In a way I am hovering above myself, and I can do things now in dance that I was never able to do before."

These memories faded and I stood up and brushed the sand off my hands. I refocused for a few moments on the present. There was nobody else around; I was completely alone. Then I took the next step, and my recollection of the years in Israel continued.

After Adi's horrendous experience and the increasing acts of terrorism, I needed to get out of the city and enter more quiet spaces. A room for rent became available near Kfar Saba, next to the stable where I was training a horse. I didn't hesitate to move to the country. Late afternoons I drove the twenty miles to the city to attend classes from 5:00 – 9:00 p.m.

When I was relying on my machine the most, the Jawa broke down, beyond repair. I felt terrified to take the bus but had no choice. Riding my motorcycle, I always passed buses as quickly as I could, aware of the need to escape the possible exploding, flaming inferno. Without my bike, I was vulnerable.

The bus line to Tel Aviv went through Petach Tikva, a transfer point for Palestinian workers from the West Bank. They came to the city for menial labor, working construction or in hotel kitchens. They carried their belongings in heavy bags, staying in the city for a week at a time, sharing rooms with a dozen other workers. They looked sad and kept to themselves, avoiding eye contact with the Israelis. In this constant state of fear, everyone tensed up when a Palestinian entered the bus. Armed soldiers patrolled buses, but we knew that there wasn't enough military power to search every bus and every bag.

It was nerve racking for everyone, Israelis and Palestinians alike.

Desperately I had searched for a motorcycle fitting my modest budget. Two weeks later I found a Suzuki GSX 400. The bike was shiny black with a red stripe across the fuel tank. Its maximum speed peaked at ninety-five miles per hour. The handle bars were crooked due to a previous accident. I rode the machine awkwardly in its injured state for an entire month until saving enough money for the repair. I loved the bike. Its exhaust howled a powerful deep roar. Compared to the Jawa, the Suzuki offered a sophisticated riding experience, traveling fast while looking streamlined and elegant.

This motorcycle created countless fond memories: Once, on the Jewish holiday of Lag Ba'Omer, I visited friends in Haifa, the port city in Northern Israel. At nightfall, I had returned home taking the coastal highway. A slim moon and a few stars sparkled above. The salty scent of the Mediterranean Sea streamed into my lungs. Prepared for a ride through the dark, I zipped up my leather jacket protecting myself from the cold. With no other traffic around, I enjoyed my solitude. I opened the throttle and the bike leaped forward.

I left Haifa behind quickly, only to be surprised by an unexpected sight of hundreds of bonfires lit along the beach. People were celebrating the Jewish holiday. Glimmering silhouettes of people moved around the flames. I felt a sense of timelessness. The wind blew flaming sparks toward the heavens. My mind catapulted back in time to an era when fire served as a tool for communication from village to village. Miles later the towering ruins of the crusader castle Atlit were outlined in the distance. Massive tall stonewalls, framed by an indigo sky and a dark sea, stood as a reminder of the crusaders' last stronghold in the Holy Land. A shiver ran up my spine; I felt humbled by the weight of history.

On another night, while returning from Jerusalem to Tel Aviv, the highway led through the mountains, and I enjoyed descending the high slopes. A delicious scent of pine trees invigorated me. At maximum speed, my bike rolled easily through smooth and winding curves. The wind whistled a gentle melody inside my helmet. Only six miles out of Jerusalem near the Arab town Abu Gosh, the view opened and the land stretched out like dark silk all the way thirty miles to the coast. The Mediterranean Sea reached to the horizon in the deepest color of cobalt blue. My mind turned still and clear, and the sky surrounded me in a luminous, lucid ultramarine, still holding onto the last light of day hours after the sun had set. I grasped a sense of eternal beauty, and even now this memory urges my heart to beat faster.

The labyrinth's winding path had brought me again closer to the center. I was aware of the illusion. It appeared that only a few pathways separated me from the place of balance and peace. But in reality, I was many steps away and still moving farther off. I walked on and my mind focused on a different time, in early 1997. I saw myself at a friend's house; we were hanging out and drinking beer. My Israeli boyfriend Eiran had his arm wrapped around me. The thought of Eiran brought a deep longing. I saw his big smile, his dark brown eyes, and his cute, round face. He was warm and affectionate and tried to hold on to me, but in the end I would leave him.

The TV was running in the background, and suddenly a newsflash came on. We stopped the conversation and Offer, our host, turned up the volume.

The correspondent was reporting the worst air disaster in Israeli history. Two helicopters had crashed into each other flying a night mission at the Lebanon border in Northern Israel, near Sha'ar Yishuv. Seventy-three soldiers had been killed.

Eiran turned quiet, his hand grabbed mine. Every one of our five friends talked and discussed the horrible accident. Then Eiran said, "My cousin Assaf is an elite fighter, patrolling the Safety Corridor to Lebanon. He often flies night missions. I hope he wasn't on one of the helicopters." We didn't stay much longer, went home and later that night the phone rang. Assaf was dead.

Only a couple of weeks earlier, I had seen Assaf on the news. His unit had suffered significant losses; many of his friends had been killed in action. At twenty-one, Assaf was tall and lanky, his heart abundant with youthful enthusiasm and his brown eyes rich with passion. When asked how he felt about going back to the Safety Corridor to face the threat of being ambushed and killed, he emphasized with a tranquil and determined voice: "This is my duty. If we don't do it, nobody is going to do it!"

I attended Assaf's shiva, the seven day period of mourning in the Jewish tradition. Family, friends and neighbors gathered at his home in Tel Aviv. The apartment was crowded with people. Many mourners waited outside the building on the sidewalk. Assaf's room was crammed full with friends, sitting on his bed and the floor. Eiran and I were in the living room together with around thirty people. The news channel repeatedly replayed the fallen hero's interview. Assaf's mother, aunts and his sister Shiri all cried out in grief, interrupting the continuous murmur of spoken prayers. They were all dressed in black. Tears streamed down their faces. It was heartbreaking and at the same time I noticed how much Shiri resembled her brother. She was tall and had the same dark passionate eyes.

Then the door opened and a young girl, maybe nineteen or twenty, entered the room. Pretty red hair fell in short waves to her shoulders; she wore jeans and a black blouse. Timidly she looked at everyone and then walked over to the only empty chair next to the TV set. She sat down silently and held back her tears as she stared at the barren marble tiled floor. I wondered who she was since nobody seemed to recognize her, and she didn't mingle with Assaf's friends. I asked Eiran, and he shook his head; he hadn't met her before. Half an hour later Assaf's mother took the seat next to her. They talked quietly, and then hugged and cried.

The girl and Assaf had been dating. He had kept this secret, wanting to surprise his family. The evening before Assaf had embarked onto the helicopter, he had asked her to come to Tel Aviv so that he could introduce her properly as his girlfriend.

She had come by bus, all alone, from a small town in Northern Israel. She wanted to mourn together with his parents, siblings and friends, adding the tragic ache of a young love lost.

In the fall of 1997, I completed my studies at Mahut. I had considered opening my own healing practice in Tel Aviv, but it was a big step to take, and I felt torn between my country of origin and Israel. The constant threat of terrorism not only drained me but also made me wonder if I could see myself in Israel for the rest of my life. As time went by, the thought of moving back to Germany became more appealing. I needed to figure things out and receive clarity about what to do next.

Finally, I decided to leave Israel and to leave Eiran. I sold the Suzuki to a young soldier, a new immigrant from Russia. His father, a friendly man with soft eyes, picked up the bike. Proudly he smiled and said, "I rode a motorcycle all my life in Russia. Now I am buying my son's first bike."

Later when I phoned my friends in Tel Aviv, they reported seeing the bike zoom by, easily identifying it by the red-striped black tank and the loud deep roar of its exhaust. My journey continued elsewhere, without a bike, for the years to come. But deep inside, I felt as if part of my soul would never leave Israel.

23

Walking into the shade of winding branches of a California Oak I paused. The distance to the center appeared far, but in a labyrinth one never knew. Enlightenment could be at hand any given moment. I kneeled and scooped sand into my palms, then let it flow. The tiny crystals returned to the earth. 'Dust to Dust,' I thought.

My years in Israel had taught me to never take anything for granted, not life, not people. Without guarantees of a tomorrow, one learned the essentials: to love as much as possible, to make this world a better place, to create peace and to never wait to live our dreams. The unbound appreciation for life and for being alive filled my heart, and slowly I continued my walk, reflecting upon life's mystifying unfolding.

Reaching the labyrinth's exit completed my walk. Inspired by good thoughts, I took a seat on the bench, enjoying the silence and overlooking the sacred circle. During my teenage years, I had wondered who I would become and how my life would turn out. At forty, I felt blessed for this fantastic journey. My life was getting better with every day. I longed to travel back in time and whisper words of confidence, wisdom and reassurance into the teenager's ears, to advise her to listen to her heart and to never stop dreaming. But then, who knew? Maybe I had listened to the whisper all along, my higher self always pulling me toward the fulfillment of my loftiest dreams.

The nun, who had welcomed me the evening before, walked by, dressed in a long black skirt and a long-sleeved beige blouse, buttoned to her neck. She nodded.

"This labyrinth is very powerful," I said.

"Yes, it's beautiful and draws in many people. But I don't appreciate the phallic symbol in the middle," she answered.

Astonished, I looked over to the erect monolith. The changing sunlight colored the rock in bronze, emphasizing its sacredness. Gilad's teachings about subjective reality came to mind. To me the center stone anchored the beacon of light, connecting heaven and earth; the nun perceived a phallus, and someone else may have seen something entirely different. Shaped by our experiences, we give meaning to all objects. Nothing is ever as it appears and nothing has meaning on its own.

Friday, August 25th. My friend Erin arrived early afternoon from Pittsburgh. She pulled up to the Mercy Center's front entrance in a rental car. I had been waiting, sitting in the sun, and when I saw her, I jumped up. A playful smile enlightened Erin's heart-shaped face. She pushed her sunglasses onto her head of dark brown shoulder length hair, revealing blue-green sparkling eyes. We hugged, happy to see each other. Erin, the second born of five daughters of a big Irish family, was easy-going, always up for some good fun and lived her life according to her favorite motto 'Keep it real.' We had first met three years ago while she was going through a difficult life transition. Her sister Kerry had registered her for my meditation class, suggesting she should become friends with me so that we could all hang out together. Since I was single and alone in the States, her family had generously invited me to their holiday celebrations, making me feel welcome and at home.

Erin had stayed at our farm in Germany, joining my 39th birthday party. I felt a special bond to the first American friend who visited Rees, my hometown. The puzzle pieces of my life had unfolded primarily in three countries. None of the pieces connected. I had lived different lives and played different roles in every place. Israel, the boiling melting pot signified by its passionate intensity, weighed as the opposing force to the moderate German and American temperament.

"I am starved," Erin said in her attractive voice. "Let's go and get something to eat." We packed my luggage into the trunk and drove off.

I turned my head once to check the bike, safely protected under a brand-new cover, purchased the day before while the machine had received an oil-change at a dealership nearby. The nuns were allowing me to leave the motorcycle for four days in their gated parking lot while Erin and I would venture off to San Francisco and Monterey Bay.

We drove a few miles to Burlingame's lively streets, parked the car and discovered an empty outdoor table at a small restaurant. Laughter and conversations from the neighboring tables surrounded us. Erin ordered wine while I opted for a local brew to toast our vacation.

"I need to try this beer," I said, lifting the cold glass to my mouth. "On the way from Sacramento I drove behind an Anchor Steam Beer truck. It was the toughest ride so far and I totally longed for a cold beer at the end of a rough day. But the nuns don't permit alcohol on their premises."

Erin burst out laughing showing her cute dimples. "And you wanted us to stay with the nuns the entire time!"

While planning the trip, I had sent Erin the web-link to the Sisters of Mercy. Not impressed, she refused to stay at a convent and made reservations for a double room at the Westin St. Francis in downtown San Francisco.

"Yes, I know. I got my spiritual fix and some relaxation, and now we can focus on pleasure and sightseeing," I said.

"And walking labyrinths. I can't wait to walk the labyrinth at Grace Cathedral," Erin added.

We toasted in German, "Prost."

Later, satisfied after a good meal, we got back into the car, heading downtown. Erin turned on the radio. Mick Jagger's voice roared over the speakers. "You can't always get what you want. But if you try sometimes, well you just might find, you get what you need." Our favorite Rolling Stones' song reaffirmed the meaningfulness of our journey. We sang cheerfully to the tunes. Erin tapped her finger tips rhythmically on the steering wheel.

In my meditation classes, I teach about synchronicities and the creative ways the intangible world communicates with us. The physical realm is just a small fraction of all creation. For the majority of us, the manifest world is our only reality; however we just may be like babies. When a baby is born his whole world contains nothing but the nursery, the apartment, the small world he may be exposed to. Then the child grows and the world he lives in expands, but still he has no idea of the vastness of the world. He grows up and travels and his concept of reality develops. In spirituality it is the same. As we awaken spiritually, we are like babies, not aware of the enormity of the world beyond. But over time, if it's our desire, we learn to connect to the upper worlds. The intangible, non-physical realm communicates with us at all times.

When Erin had taken the class, she noticed that every time she found herself unhappy or struggling with life's challenges, she heard this song playing on the radio, on the TV, in the mall, wherever she was at that moment. It told her again and again, "You can't always get what you want, but you always get what you need." First she thought it was weird magic, but eventually she realized that this purposeful coincidence allowed her to shift awareness and see that her life situation at that time was exactly what she needed for her inner growth.

We approached Union Square, and I enjoyed the multicultural cosmopolitan character, a nice contrast after two days of seclusion in the convent's sanctuary. Sidewalks were filled with people and the notes of a saxophone player streamed through the open window into our car. Then we checked in at the legendary St. Francis, walked through the luxurious lobby past a fine art gallery and an expensive jewelry store and took the elevator to the 11th floor. The deluxe room featured two queen-sized beds. We threw ourselves onto the feather comforters, and linen, soft as velvet, caressed our skin.

"Good choice, Erin," I said. "Thanks for not listening to me."

"I bet you are not going to fall out of this bed like you did during your first night at the Mercy Center," she responded.

"No, definitely not." We laughed.

Erin showered and changed, freshening up from the four hour flight. Then we explored the neighborhood. Walking up a long hill, we arrived at a number of bars and restaurants. The first place attracted my attention; the windows were covered with Pittsburgh Steelers paraphernalia. Its logo read, "Giordano Bros."

"Hey, Erin, check it out. A Steelers bar. Isn't that a funny coincidence?"

"Cool, let's go in."

We sat at the bar and ordered drinks.

"What's the connection to Pittsburgh?" Erin asked the bartender.

"The owners went to Allegheny College in PA."

"I went to Allegheny College," Erin said.

"The band that plays tonight, some of the guys also studied at Allegheny."

We turned our heads to the musicians, who were setting up their instruments.

"Oh my God," Erin said. "I know them. I haven't seen them in years."

We spent the evening listening to alternative rock. During the performance breaks, Erin and her friends shared college anecdotes. We also learned that the Giordano Bros. menu was based on the famous Primanti Bros. menu in Pittsburgh.

Later Erin and I returned to the hotel. I tried to phone Frank, excited to tell him about the Steelers bar. He didn't answer. I shook my head. "I don't understand. He insisted that I get the phone so that we could talk every day, and now he doesn't answer. It's the second day in a row."

"That's weird," Erin said and shrugged her shoulders.

"Yes. And now I'm upset that he doesn't even think to call me. I should never have gotten the damn phone. Just should have done this whole trip my way. Thank God that I didn't allow him to come with me."

"He wanted to come with you on this trip?" Erin asked. "You never told me that."

"Yes. That was one of the first things he said when we started dating. He thought it was so cool. But there was no way he was joining me for the entire journey. First, I hardly knew him and I had planned this trip before we met. There are certain things you have to do alone. This is all about turning 40, and reflecting on my life, and figuring out where I am going from here. If you travel with another person, especially if it's your lover, you can't figure things out. You're too focused on each other."

"I am glad, then, that I am allowed to travel with you." Erin burst out laughing and threw me a pillow.

"Men may come and go. Girlfriends are forever," I said, also laughing, and threw the pillow back.

"Sure, but then he's still coming out to L.A.; when does he arrive?" Erin asked and threw the pillow back at me."

"September 3rd. He already scheduled job interviews. It feels all right that we move out West together. At least that's the plan. But I am not sure if the relationship will fulfill me in the long run. We'll see. Life is big and a lot of things can happen," I concluded.

24

The morning of August 26th, Erin and I walked up the steep Jones Street to Nob Hill and Grace Cathedral. Designed in magnificent French gothic architecture, the cathedral stood as a timeless monument amidst white modern high rises.

A vision of Bishop Nichols, it had been built after the disaster of the 1906 earthquake. Citywide fires had destroyed Grace church and the Crocker mansions. William Crocker, a banker and philanthropist, and his father, Charles Crocker, a transcontinental railroad builder, had donated the entire city block for the Episcopal house of prayer.

We entered through the main entrance underneath two massive 174-foot tall façade towers. Abruptly cut off from the outside world, spirited organ music embraced us. My heart trembled to the overture's intensity. My eyes adjusted to the dimmed cave-like light. Stained glass windows soared 40 feet tall and filtered into rays of aquamarine and red. High above the altar, the facetted round window looked down on the humble parishioners like the eye of God.

The woolen labyrinth tapestry covered the stone floor in the cathedral's nave. Outlined in a soft mauve on the off-white ground the 11-circuit medieval labyrinth pattern invited a sacred experience.[2]

'This is where the popularization of the ancient spiritual tool began,' I thought. In 1991 Dr. Lauren Artess, then Canon Pastor at Grace Cathedral, had first experienced the power of the labyrinth at Jean Houston's Mystery School. She then traveled to France and brought the 11-circuit labyrinth pattern from the Chartres Cathedral near Paris to San Francisco. The labyrinth's wisdom attracted many followers and a movement of awakening had been born.

I had anticipated this labyrinth as being the road trip's highlight. But I was feeling hesitant. Seven people circled to and away from the center. None of them were absorbed by the labyrinth's holiness. A couple in their mid-fifties both held cameras and frequently stopped to take pictures. A younger couple chatted while looking around at other people. The other three hurried, without any depth or reflection.

'Was this the dark side of the labyrinth's celebrity status?' I wondered. A mystical experience requires cultivation, introspection and patience. A labyrinth can't be easily consumed like fast food. There is no quick spiritual fix, no short cuts to enlightenment. The labyrinth gives us only as much as we invest. The greater our dedication, the greater the benefit.

Erin shook her head and said, "Let's go and take a look around." We walked to the main floor lobby of the cathedral's north tower and admired the AIDS quilt. The colorful patchwork was created as a memorial to those who had died of AIDS and to honor the caregivers and volunteers who fight HIV, despite decades of prejudice, resistance and apathy. Then we strolled to the acrylic murals, depicting the cathedral's history and the founding of the United Nations in San Francisco in 1945.

The organ music played uninterruptedly but then changed to a slower pace. I closed my eyes. My mind was impressed with exceptional art and streams of colors floated in front of my inner eye. I felt energized and uplifted. I have rarely entered this ecstatic state of consciousness, and then only when I see good art in museums and galleries, or when I paint.

I turned and saw the labyrinth had emptied. Erin smiled, "Good, now we can walk it." By the time we reached the nave, two women stood at the labyrinth's entrance. They looked like sisters, delicate cheekbones, and pale lips, both in their late forties. The older sister had dressed in an emerald skirt and a white knit sweater; her blond hair fell to her shoulders. The other woman wore fashionable, elegant pants, a blouse, red shoes and gold earrings. Both women were thin and seemed fragile. They bowed and then entered the sacred circle, staying close together. I didn't see their eyes; they stared at the floor, away from the living. I sensed they mourned the loss of a loved one. Erin and I waited a few minutes, and then we took off our shoes and joined.

The sisters proceeded at a slow pace in deep contemplation. From time to time, the older one tucked her hair nervously behind her ears. We passed them respectfully. I wondered about the heavy burden they carried; it seemed they never saw us, locked in their own despair-filled universe. A sense of pain spread through the labyrinth. Erin felt it, too. Ahead of me she paused, looked into my eyes, placed her hand on her heart and exhaled. We continued in silence.

Three young men lined up at the labyrinth's entrance. In their early twenties they were dressed in jeans, flip flops and T-shirts, all blond and handsome. One by one they bowed and zoomed into the labyrinth. Instantly the cloud lifted and a fresh breeze streamed in. The heaviness evaporated. They passed us and reached the center. Clockwise they entered the six petals and then moved out as quickly as they had entered. These young men knew exactly what they were doing. I felt their reverence for the labyrinth; they traveled at light speed, in tune with the higher forces, and they had arrived at the perfect moment. In sync with us, the organ music changed to light-hearted tunes, pointing out the shift.

The sisters still stared down, didn't change their pace, but their bodies looked relaxed; their shoulders raised, their chests opened.

Erin and I reached the center, entered the petals clockwise and then wandered the twists and turns out of the labyrinth. We passed the sisters and gently stepped aside. Then Erin, ahead of me, exited the labyrinth. I intended to follow but hit a wall and couldn't get out. I had become accustomed to this phenomenon; first it had happened in New Harmony and then in the Starhouse Labyrinth. I turned to the sisters, both kneeling in the center. The older sister leaned over and her forehead touched the tapestry.

I began walking the lunations clockwise and sensed that my movement kept the labyrinth's energy field spiraling. I surrendered to the process and focused on breathing in the divine light. I lost track of how many times I circled the labyrinth, ten times, twenty times; suddenly an urge swept through me and forced me to step out of the labyrinth. At that exact moment the two sisters stood up. I bowed and walked over to Erin, who had been watching.

"Unbelievable," she whispered. "You all moved at the same moment, as if orchestrated from above."

The sisters slowly journeyed out of the labyrinth, and Erin and I strolled in silence to the main entrance. Outside we were blinded by the sun and our eyes needed to adjust. We sat on a bench overlooking the outdoor labyrinth, made of terrazzo stone.

"How about those gorgeous young men? They were like gods," I said.

"Or angels. I can't believe how the energy shifted as soon as they entered," Erin answered.

"That was very powerful. I also realized that I had never walked a labyrinth with complete strangers before. We definitely needed to wait for the right moment," I said.

"This was my third walk. I walked the Westminster Labyrinth in Pittsburgh once before with you and then also on the morning you left for this trip. I truly believe in the power of the labyrinth. I meditated on letting go of past patterns. When I reached the middle and entered every petal, I wanted to focus on specific things, but it felt like they already had left me. I connected to the light and everything was clear. The path out of the labyrinth was very easy, very light and I felt so happy."

"There was also a complete sense of trust, even though we walked the labyrinth with strangers, people who we may never see again. We were all drawn to the labyrinth at the same time. And every one of us seemed respectful and knowledgeable of what the labyrinth can offer," I continued.

"Yes. And that would not have happened earlier with the people who took pictures and had no idea what they were doing. We needed to wait for the right time," Erin said.

We enjoyed the sun for a little while and then continued to explore the streets of San Francisco. In the evening Frank called and said he had been really busy. I couldn't imagine what he had been so busy with that he forgot to call me. In no mood to argue, I didn't express how I felt.

The next day Erin and I visited Fishermen's Wharf, Haight-Ashbury and then continued to Monterey. We stayed with Erin's sister's parents-in-law and enjoyed the luxury of a country club lifestyle. We hung out, relaxed and indulged in good food and excellent wine. Erin flew back to Pittsburgh on August 29th, and I picked up my bike at the Sisters of Mercy.

25

A visit to San Francisco wouldn't be complete without crossing the Golden Gate Bridge. Late morning on the 16th day of my journey, I merged into traffic. The fog lifted revealing a brilliant sky and promising a good day. I whistled lightheartedly into my helmet.

The bridge's towers stood tall, shining bright red in the sun. I rode slowly, 35 miles an hour, trying to make this experience last. To my right, the bay opened in a magnificent blue. White sailboats leaned into the wind. I turned my head to see Alcatraz and downtown San Francisco. To my left, the Pacific Ocean reached endless to the horizon, shining in mystical silver.

Crossing the Golden Gate Bridge carried a deep metaphorical meaning for me. Comparing this adventure to the three aspects of a labyrinth walk, I had reached the middle section of the road trip. The ride to the West symbolized the journey into the labyrinth, a reflection upon my past and the aspects of release and purification.

The journey along the West Coast translated into reaching the labyrinth's center, a state of inner balance, allowing me to uncover new aspects of my personality and grow into my own strength. The ride back East would represent the third part of integration and the emerging of a new, more evolved self.

I raised my head to the massive suspension cables and steel wires flickered red, gold and orange. The effect of light and motion mesmerized me, but I had to keep my eyes on the road. Focused on the moment, I simultaneously catapulted back to the Lower Rhine Valley. My hometown's neighboring city Emmerich featured the longest suspension bridge in Germany. Inspired by the Golden Gate Bridge in far away America, the bridge had been painted in the same bright red. 'After all, life just goes in circles,' I thought.

I continued on Highway 101 North toward Kentfield. Late afternoon I pulled into Penny Gerbode's driveway. She had responded to my call for labyrinths and generously invited me to stay at her home. Promptly she opened the front door and waved her hands.

In her late fifties, she radiated an aura of strength and ease. She wore her brown hair short. A white T-shirt emphasized her suntanned skin. She smiled generously; her green eyes sparkled.

"Welcome," she said. Her voice sounded like a soothing trickle of water.

We hugged and then she helped carry the luggage and directed me to the guestroom. Her house was built on a hillside surrounded by redwoods and pines. I followed Penny down the stairs through a long corridor. Ultramarine and emerald abstract paintings captured the eye.

"You'll have this entire floor to yourself. My room is upstairs," she said.

Later we drove to Sonoma's historical city center, and Penny turned right to the Trinity Episcopal Church. The wooden building charmed with its simplicity. The labyrinth was laid out in river rock and encircled by 200-year-old redwoods.

We sat on a bench, protected by massive trees, and tuned into the sacred circle's beauty. The green scent of the nature sanctuary filled my lungs. The sun stood low and a soft evening light brought peace. I traced the 9-circuit path with my eyes and relaxed. Penny stood up in silence, walked to the labyrinth's entrance and started her journey. Instantly birds sang, as if to cheer us from their elevated perspective high up in the tree branches. Not compelled to join, I watched Penny as she took the twists and turns in a fluid movement.

Then I closed my eyes and quickly drifted into a trance-like state. The solid world disintegrated in front of my inner eye. I saw swirling patterns of light and energy. I felt grounded to the earth and at the same time, a tingling sensation stimulated the top of my head, as if my mind had blown wide open. I perceived a vision of Hebrew letters flickering out of the swirls of light and then dissolving, turning into light again. My studies into the wisdom of Kabbalah had taught me that every letter of the Hebrew alphabet is considered a building block of creation. Every letter contains a numerical value. This ancient wisdom, called Gematria, evaluates relationships. For example, the numerical value of the word God is equal to the word nature. I think that God is easy to find in nature and God also expresses himself through the laws and the splendor of nature. Without walking the labyrinth, I was already in the midst of a spiritual experience.

Then a dog barked. I opened my eyes, surprised to see Penny exiting the labyrinth. I had lost my sense of time. We smiled at each other, and I proceeded to follow the winding path. A fascinating split between body and mind allowed for a new perspective. Weightless and free, my mind floated high above while I felt solid and grounded inside my physical body. A sense of ecstasy increased with every step. The large redwoods' strength protectively wrapped itself around me. I saw the trees as a metaphor for the human being. Our roots connect us to the earth; our crown reaches out to the heavens. As balanced human beings, we exist in both worlds and are able to communicate between heaven and earth.

But then suddenly my inner light vanished. Anchored in my body, I felt heavy and for a moment I couldn't breathe. My mind catapulted right back into the life review, which I had started during the labyrinth walk at the Sisters of Mercy in Burlingame. Images flashed like snapshots. I had left Israel and moved back to Germany. It was spring 1998. I lived in Düsseldorf. Two art shows called 'Retrospective of the Years in Israel' and 'Passion of Colors' had sold most of my abstract oil paintings. Despite this success I wasn't inspired to create new art. I felt empty. At the same time, I tried to build a business with reflexology and was working part-time at the airport, profiling passengers for a security firm, a job I had found through an Israeli friend.

I saw airplanes take off every day, and as the months passed, my hunger for travel and adventure grew. I missed the Mediterranean warm-hearted openness, the spontaneity and the ease of flow. Not afraid, Israelis freely shared their innermost feelings and thoughts. In my mind, the intensity of everyday life unified people at their core. There was nothing to hide, nothing to be ashamed of and nothing taboo.

Once, I had traveled by bus in Tel Aviv and a middle aged woman sitting in front of me had turned to her neighbor gushing on about her marital problems. Soon everybody joined the conversation, pitched in ideas, gave suggestions and talked about their own difficulties.

Complete strangers engaged in a most intimate discussion. This was the norm. I had experienced this over and over again. Initially, it had felt strange. But I learned to value the freedom and trust it takes to open your heart to strangers. The consequent insight emerged that as human beings all our struggles and emotions are quite alike. To share ourselves freely with our fellow human beings unburdens the soul and allows us to live an authentic life without shame or the concern of what others may say.

In Düsseldorf, I went by bus to the airport. Day after day, my fellow passengers sat still in their seats, kept to themselves, stiff and rigid and strictly avoided eye contact.

Then my mind zoomed in on a particular moment at the Düsseldorf airport. My shift was done, my co-workers had left, but I had stayed behind, taken a seat next to large windows and watched airplanes lift up into the typical German grey sky. My hair was still short, hadn't grown much since I cut it off to mark the return to my homeland. I had intended to symbolize the next chapter in my life with a new look, then still filled with anticipation and excitement. But several months had passed, and my younger self didn't show any expression of happiness. I was dressed in a dark blue uniform, a white buttoned-up blouse and a red-blue-striped scarf neatly wrapped around my neck. As I watched airplane after airplane take off, my frustration about my life in Germany grew. I had felt that I had reached a dead end and made up my mind. Loud and clear I said, "I am out of here."

I stood up, phoned my boss and announced my resignation. Late afternoon I cancelled the lease for my one bedroom apartment. I had given myself thirty days until I would return to Israel.

I stopped. The labyrinth was peaceful. Penny sat on a bench; her eyes were closed. I assumed she was in deep meditation. I let my gaze wander upward and slowly felt my chest open. The labyrinth was shaded, but the sun gently illuminated the redwoods' crowns. Then I took the next step and jolted back to Düsseldorf. I saw myself in a restaurant with Paul, the American man whom I had been dating for less than half a year. Over dinner I told him my plans and he was shocked.

"What will happen to us when you move to the Middle East?" he asked.

I shrugged my shoulders. "I don't know."

"Marry me and come with me to America!" he said.

His proposal took me by surprise. We didn't know each other well. Paul worked in the airline industry and we had seen each other only five or six times per month. Nine years older than I, his blond hair had aged prematurely to a silver grey. A handsome full beard framed his face, and he wore thin-rimmed glasses. In his youth, he had owned a horse. Funny and charismatic most of the time, he also easily switched to a dark seriousness, especially when I mentioned motorcycles.

"I could never tolerate it if you wanted to ride a motorcycle again. I would worry about you all the time," he said with an attractive deep voice. "When I was eight years old, I witnessed a motorcyclist crash into a tree in front of my parents' house. He was killed instantly. It was awful and I despise motorcycles."

I was in love with Paul and considered his proposal, but I also felt hesitant since I had never been to America. I asked him to give me some time to think about it and began practicing daily the decision-making-meditation.

I saw myself in my apartment, sitting in a comfortable arm chair; I was taking a few deep breaths and then closed my eyes. Simultaneously in the labyrinth, eight years later, I stood still, closed my eyes and relived every part of this meditation, exactly the way it occurred then. I focused on breathing in divine light and exhaling all tensions, concerns and worries. Within seconds, my entire body relaxed and vibrated to the rhythm of the divine light. I focused my mind on happy memories and entered a state of joy, sensing feelings of protection and love in this world. I smiled.

Then I visualized myself embarking on a journey through nature. Saturated with joy and ease, I expected the best. Gracefully, I walked the golden path, which allowed me to tune into my life's mission. I reached a junction and decided where to turn. In my meditation, I safely explored both ways. The path leading back to Israel was filled with obstacles. I encountered big rocks and boulders obstructing the way. My sense of ease and joy evaporated. Dark violent clouds filled the sky. It felt impossible to continue my journey to Israel. Then I stumbled and couldn't breathe.

As soon as I turned to America, the sky opened into a bright and brilliant blue. Warm sunrays caressed my skin, birds sang and beautiful fields of flowers surrounded me. I walked the golden path filled with blessings and joy.

151

I received the same message two dozen times and then I talked to Paul. He was ecstatic when I said, "Yes."

I opened my eyes and stepped forward. I wasn't far from the labyrinth's center. The next puzzle pieces of my life showed themselves in quick snippets, not leaving time to linger or for emotions to surface.

In May 1998, I arrived in Pittsburgh, Pennsylvania. Only two weeks later, my father suddenly died of complications after an emergency surgery on his colon. Devastated, I traveled back to Germany for his funeral. The family and friends, with whom we had just celebrated my farewell party, now gathered at his grave.

Weeks later, I returned to Pittsburgh and slowly started my new life. I liked the city, the three rivers, the many bridges and the surrounding lush rolling green hills. A shining example for the transformation of a polluted steel city to an inviting modern day metropolis, Pittsburgh attracted high tech businesses and featured the country's best hospitals.

I joined a team of skilled holistic practioners and offered reflexology and meditation courses at the Center for Integrative Medicine at the University of Pittsburgh Medical Center. Our medical director, Dr. David Servan-Schreiber, was a pioneering Frenchman and author of the ground-breaking books *Instinct to Heal – Curing stress, anxiety and depression without drugs and without talk therapy* and *Anticancer: A New Way of Life*. For me, a dream was coming true, to see scientific and holistic medicine effectively melding together for the highest good of the patient.

Then, four years later, my relationship with Paul fell apart. I had considered moving back to Europe but didn't want to give up a thriving career. I decided to stay, regardless of the divorce. I knew if things didn't work out, I could always return to Europe.

Being single again translated into fulfilling my biggest dream; I yearned to ride a motorcycle. Missing the freedom and adventure, I had also discovered a new aspect. Since I owned a car, a bike was not a necessity or a means of affordable transportation, like in Israel. The cold snowy Pittsburgh winters would only allow me to ride during summer. For the first time a motorcycle meant to satisfy a desire for pure pleasure.

As a special gift, I bought a brand new Suzuki Bandit 600 motorcycle for my thirty-sixth birthday. I loved its iridescent brilliant blue color. Thinking of my perfect vehicle I reached the labyrinth's center.

26

August 30th, day seventeen, I traveled south. Heavy fog clouded the Golden Gate Bridge. Invisible below, the open bay intensified the ice-cold dampness. I reached the other side and freezing shivers ran up my spine. In the flow with morning traffic I didn't stop to put on rain gear. Instead I pressed on. Only a hundred miles later near Monterey, the fog that had hugged the coast finally lifted. Scenic Route 1 revealed itself in all its beauty. The tarmac wound through rugged canyons and steep sea cliffs fell straight to granite shorelines. I zoomed past Big Sur's enormous redwoods and continued on a solitary ride along the Pacific. A warm breeze caressed my face as I pushed my visor open. The scent of ocean mist and sandy beaches filled my lungs. A brilliant haze hovered on top of turquoise water. White foam rose above the waves. To the east hilly formations of scorched uninhabited land looked like sleeping pre-historic reptiles.

At 2:30 p.m. I took the Avila Beach exit and then slowed down into the parking lot at the Sycamore Mineral Springs Resort. The young woman at the reception desk directed me to the labyrinth. I left the bike fully loaded close to the main entrance, trusting that nobody would touch my belongings. A pedestrian bridge led across Avila Beach Drive and San Luis Creek to the meditation garden. Sunflowers lined the walkway. Hundreds of golden yellow heads turned to the sun. Bees buzzed and crickets chirped.

Tucked away at the outer edge of the property, the labyrinth was nestled in an oasis of white sycamores. I took a seat on a wooden bench, overlooking the impressive sacred circle, and estimated its dimension at 60 feet. The 11-circuit design was laid out in river rock. Oval rocks stood upright, halfway embedded in stomped earth. The massive number of stones created an aura of abundance. I felt grounded. My thoughts drifted to various subjects for my exploration. I asked myself what I needed to work on to become a better person and to grow spiritually. A flash of insight revealed the answer. The labyrinth invited me to focus on the source of my inner strength.

I took off my heavy boots and placed them side by side next to the entrance. While taking my first turns into the sacred circle, I suddenly felt compelled to look back. I stared at my carefully arranged black biker boots. The moment I had stepped out of them I had stripped off a part of my identity, a persona that could be tough and determined. Now I was unarmored and vulnerable. I contemplated that one day I would step out of my body, too, and leave it behind like a garment.

The air stood still, as if holding its breath. Barefoot, I continued on my solitary path. At the third turn I stopped. Startled, I perceived a gentle wave of density spinning around me. A slight breeze moved the air. The labyrinth felt animated, as if I were not alone. I moved on and attempted to focus my mind on 'inner strength,' repeating the words like a mantra. Still, I was distracted by this unusual occurrence. What was going on? What did this mean? In response to my thoughts the presence of two forces emerged next to me. It felt as if they took me into their arms and provided guidance. Not scared, I focused on my breathing. At the seventh turn, I closed my eyes.

And then, finally, I saw. The dense energies that I had sensed revealed themselves as my grandmothers. They were right there with me. We had never met. Both had died decades ago, but I had seen their pictures. I felt safe and protected, as I held the image of these two strong women accompanying me. My mom's mother had her long grey hair pulled up, tied together in a knot. Her striking face looked soft with age. Her calm smile brought confidence. She wore elegant pearl earrings, a grey woolen skirt and a fine white blouse.

My dad's mother was a robust, vigorous farm woman. Streaks of her natural black color accentuated her greying hair, also pulled back into a knot. She wore black, like one would wear to a funeral, to represent the grief in her life. The pain she had suffered did not diminish her force. She had been a determined woman who would fight for anything that was hers and anything that she was devoted to.

She sent a stream of brilliant light from her heart into my heart. An expansive sensation of peace and love warmed my chest. I turned my head left and perceived my maternal grandmother sending a stream of deep love, sweet and bright, containing the essence of all lessons she had learned in life. Her message advised softness and surrender. Softness, like flowing water, which swiftly moves around obstacles and finds a new way. Surrender, like a young tree that easily bends to the direction of the wind. The tree's flexibility keeps it from breaking. My heart opened. I advanced on my path, thrilled to be accompanied by two great women.

I arrived at the labyrinth's center and an immense sense of strength filled me. There was another presence that I felt. With my eyes open I saw nothing, but when I closed my eyes, I received the image of my parents standing in front of me. My previous perception of colors ceased. Something within me shifted and became brighter. In the labyrinth's center I saw my parents in their light bodies. My inner eye saw the clear image of my parents, emerging out of pulsing fields of light. They smiled and I sensed their love. They stood a few inches taller than their actual height. Consequently, I looked up to them. Mixed emotions surfaced; I felt happy and sad at the same time. I loved my parents, but we did not always agree. Clearly I felt the grief I had caused when I moved far away from home. The labyrinth allowed us to connect on a higher level, and I realized that they wanted only the best for me. Humbled I bowed, my palms open, and turned toward my parents while my eyes remained closed. I breathed deeply for an immeasurable amount of time. Then a space inside my chest burst open, like a petal opening its blossoms to unfold its beauty. Oxygen streamed abundantly into my lungs.

I lifted my head and sensed that my grandparents stood right behind my mother and my father, sending strength, wisdom and love. They were also a few inches taller, allowing me to look into their eyes. An intimate connection bonded me to my grandmothers. My grandparents' love streamed from their hearts into my parents' hearts and then into mine. It felt as if my heart tingled. Overwhelmed by the sensation, I placed my hands on my chest, took a few deep breaths and then meditated on opening my heart to receive their love.

Quietly, I said, "Yes." My mixed emotions evaporated. Then the next generation revealed itself to me. My great-grandparents stood a few inches taller. My body trembled from the intensity of this experience. I thought that I didn't know anything about them; all were strangers to me. But their destinies were connected through the fact that I had received the gift of life through them.

I slowly connected to every generation. Each generation was bigger than the previous one. To me it looked like a bridge of love reaching to the heavens.

I felt overwhelmed by the sheer number of people. Including the seventh generation back, there had to be more than a couple hundred ancestors. I opened my eyes and tried to ground myself in the midst of this exponentially growing force. "Ask and you shall receive," I humored myself. I had intended to connect to my source of inner strength and I was surrounded by my ancestors. I did the math. In the seventh generation were 128 people. Eight generations back there were 256 people; nine generations back were 512, and ten generations back 1024.

1024 destinies. Men and women, from different backgrounds, different social classes, different countries, separated by different dialects and languages. Some were enemies, who had fought against each other in wars. Their blood was flowing in my veins. But here in my labyrinth experience, limitless love bridged the generations and transcended time and space. Nothing else mattered.

I looked around, inhaled deeply. Strong sycamore trees encircled the labyrinth. Sunshine caressed my skin and colorful butterflies danced in the air. Then I closed my eyes again and to my surprise the vision was gone. I didn't see my ancestors; I saw only intense swirling fields of light. 'It doesn't matter,' I thought. 'The vision is gone, but a seed has been planted inside my heart. What I have seen has become my truth.' I traced the path out of the labyrinth and knew that I would never be alone again. A sense of responsibility came into my consciousness. Life was a gift and I had to aspire to live my best life every moment and every day, an easy task in the presence of such strength and wisdom. I felt playful, just like a little girl.

I walked back to the meditation garden, past hundreds of sunflowers, and then crossed the bridge, got back on my bike and continued along the coast on Highway 101. Only 15 minutes later I pulled off in Pismo Beach. The Best Western Shore Cliff Lodge, located on top of a 90-foot cliff, offered a spectacular view. 'A perfect place to end a phenomenal day,' I thought. The odometer indicated that I had ridden 295 miles. I checked in, ate dinner at a nearby restaurant, and then relaxed on the porch of my room to call Frank. I was happy to hear his voice. He would arrive in a few days and then we would spend one week together to figure out our new life in Southern California.

While we talked, wild pelicans glided by, frolicking, and then circled around three palm trees at the edge of the cliff. The sun sank deeper, turning sky and ocean orange-red, later violet, then indigo. Soon after I went to bed and lullabies of ocean waves guided me into my dreams.

27

The last day of August, I woke up well rested. I did not recall my dreams but sensed that I had processed a lot of information during my sleep. I perceived a new quality of awareness. The playfulness that had come to me the previous day remained. I felt giddy, excited and light. There was no care in the world. No concerns, nothing to worry about, just the joy of being in the present moment.

I opened the drapes and stared at a solid wall of opaque fog. The ocean had disappeared. Even the sound of waves had been smothered. 'No problem,' I thought. 'Today will be a fantastic day.'

I had breakfast and by 9:00 a.m. I was back on the road, driving south. The fog only lifted temporarily when 101 turned inland to Santa Maria. As soon as I reached the Pacific at Gaviota, dense, cold fog crawled again underneath my leathers. I passed Santa Barbara and then turned onto 150 to climb into the mountains. Finally, bright hot sunshine embraced me. The two-lane road wound higher, and I turned my head once to see white fog, like snow rolling in from the ocean. Then I crossed a ridge, and spectacular mountain ranges and the zigzag shaped turquoise Lake Casitas spread out in front of me. The scent of pine and sage streamed into my lungs. The air was dry and the sky, empty of all clouds, reached up into bright blue infinity.

Two years ago, when I started planning this road trip, I had decided that turning 40 would be the right time to move to a new place. I had meditated on where I would live and slowly the message revealed itself. I had sensed I would be in California, inspired by my desire to ride a motorcycle all year round, just like I did in Israel. East Coast winters and shoveling snow had not been appealing. Slowly my attention was drawn toward Ojai. A friend gave me an Ojai visitor brochure, praising the little town as the nicest place she had stayed at on a recent West Coast trip. In a Pittsburgh restaurant people at a neighboring table had talked about Ojai. A meditation student had lived in Ojai and loved the community. A pattern emerged: Wherever I turned, Ojai was mentioned. In my daily meditations, I had tuned into the energies of my future place of residence. I consistently received a positive confirmation and, sight unseen, had made up my mind to start a new life in Ojai.

I enjoyed the ride along Lake Casitas. Fifteen minutes later, I arrived in town. I was not disappointed. Ojai was snuggled in a valley, surrounded by the Topa Topa Mountains' tall serrated peaks. The city center was built in Spanish architecture; a historic post office tower, dotted with tile, emanated the flair of Mexican cathedrals. I drove along a picturesque arcade featuring shops and art galleries. The atmosphere felt relaxed and inspiring. I turned off the main avenue, circled onto side roads, drove around, stopped at a metaphysical store on North Montgomery Street and received the recommendation to visit Meditation Mount. I rode on past a golf course to my right and endless orange groves to my left and then turned onto a one-lane road twisting uphill. I parked the bike near the retreat center and followed the path to the Garden of Peace.

White and orange wildflowers emanated a delicate, fresh scent. I strolled past cactuses, agaves and a yellow flowering thorn bush. One purple cactus stood separate and alone. I listened to the calming sound of water dripping into a pond. Bulky rocks, four feet high, lined the sandy trail. The engraved words invited meaningful contemplation. I read the inscriptions: The Path, Right Human Relations, Goodwill, Group Endeavor, Unanimity, Spiritual Approach, and Essential Divinity.

I reached a terrace of green grass. The Ojai Valley opened before me in lush splendor. The sun stood high and the air brimmed with energy. I heard bees humming. Hawks soared up into the sky, drawing patient, graceful spirals. I reclined on velvet grass, looked up to the heavens and saw specks of light flashing, dancing to the backdrop of brilliant blue. I drifted off quickly and lost my sense of time.

The approach of footsteps brought me back to the moment. A Mexican worker walked by. He carried a rake. His suntanned skin looked like aged leather. A frayed straw hat shaded his face. He smiled bright and friendly. I got up, returned to my bike and thought, 'This is a good place to be.'

Back in Ojai, I stopped at a realtor's office, picked up an information brochure about places for rent and ate a late lunch at the local health food store, Rainbowbridge. Then I descended 15 miles of delightful, mountainous slopes to the coastal city Ventura and checked into a nice hotel at the harbor. Late afternoon I hopped back on the bike. Now free of luggage, it was light and easy to navigate. I opened the throttle on 101 and sped off to Santa Barbara for a little sightseeing. The invigorating aroma of the sea flooded my lungs and I watched surfers as they rode on perfect waves. The uniqueness of the landscape amazed me; the Santa Ynez Mountains ran parallel to the Pacific Coast.

Suddenly a chill rushed through my body, a memory surfaced and instantly I transcended time and space. I saw myself back in January 2003 returning from Melbourne, Australia. In Los Angeles I had had a connecting flight to Pittsburgh. However, our landing in L.A. had been delayed and the plane diverted, and we circled over the coast into the Santa Barbara area. I had looked down onto the landscape, impressed by its beauty, and decided that one day I would ride my motorcycle on the coastal highway. The moment I had made that decision chills had rushed through me, like an inner knowing, confirming the premonition of my destiny.

Thrilled and empowered I realized that this forgotten dream had come true.

Frank arrived on Sunday morning, September 3rd. He had flown into Los Angeles and rented a car for one week. The moment I looked into his eyes and felt his hands touch my skin all previous concerns about our relationship evaporated. I noticed that I had easily thrown myself into an inner tantrum of negative self-talk, reasoning why this relationship couldn't last. Every time this thought process was triggered by him not picking up the phone or being unreachable for a couple of days. I argued that he was younger than I, that he had never traveled anywhere outside the United States, that he was too flirtatious and that he didn't take things as seriously as I did. But as he hugged me and said, "I love you so much," I wanted to believe he was right for me. And of course, Frank rode a motorbike.

We had one week to figure out the basics for our new life in California. Frank had scheduled job interviews and we needed to find an apartment. One of the first things on our agenda was to walk a labyrinth. I discovered two labyrinths in Ventura. One at the St. Paul's Episcopal Church on Loma Vista Road and the other at the First United Methodist Church on Santa Clara Street. We checked out both and Frank chose to walk the Santa Clara labyrinth.

He took a few deep breaths, tuned into the labyrinth's field and then said, "Let's walk this one. It feels warm and welcoming. It has a nice energy to it." The earth-colored labyrinth was embedded in the courtyard and surrounded by mission style buildings. A white church tower overlooked the red-shingled roof.

Robert Ferre, founder of Labyrinth Enterprises in St. Louis, Missouri, had built this labyrinth. A massive olive tree stood solidly next to the labyrinth. Frank estimated it to be more than 100 years old. I walked over and leaned into its trunk. My fingers caressed the rugged bark. A crown of silver-green leaves spread untamed in all directions. A white peace pole read in eight different languages "May Peace Prevail on Earth."

Frank skipped to the labyrinth's entrance and opened his arms toward me. "Come on, let's do it. I am ready," he said. I laughed and recalled how quickly Frank had become a convinced labyrinth enthusiast. He had never meditated before we met. Curious and intrigued, he had been eager to learn new skills. And consequently he loved to walk labyrinths regularly.

"Dorit, what are you waiting for?" he asked.

"Just thinking."

"Stop thinking, you are always in your head," he said and playfully skipped back to me. He kissed my forehead, pretended that he could magically make my thoughts disappear, then took my hand and together we walked to the labyrinth's entrance.

Frank entered in silence, but I wasn't ready yet to join and walked the lunations clockwise. Water trickled from a fountain. The olive tree stood tall and strong. I wondered about the events and people it had witnessed in 100 years. Everything in life is put into perspective by time. Life doesn't always make sense. Often the pieces of the puzzle don't connect. Only with time and reflection can we understand.

Frank threw me a kiss. I saw it as a cue to embark on my own journey into the labyrinth. Thoughts flooded my mind. 'Ask and you shall receive,' I thought. 'What did I want to ask for?' I wondered. There were of course all the practical aspects of life that needed to be fulfilled: a place to live, work, health, joy, but that was not enough. I yearned for more.

Frank walked next to me. With a few steps he reached the center. I was just at the beginning of my journey. We were separated by a fine line. We were on different paths. He reached out to hold my hand. His blue eyes looked puzzled. We connected for a moment and then moved apart into different directions.

I desired to manifest a happy and fulfilled life, a life that was deeply satisfying and truly expressed who I was. I didn't receive a concrete image, but rather a sensation, a vibration of light. I asked to come in alignment with my destiny and focused on exhaling all beliefs and perceptions that didn't serve my highest good.

By the time I reached the center, Frank was on his way out. We passed each other respectfully, bowed in front of each other. To me it felt as if we bowed to each other's destiny. His fingers gently touched my arm. A wave of love extended from my heart to his. Then I stepped into the center. My mind cleared. After a while my gaze searched for Frank; he had left the labyrinth and wandered off.

Within three days, we signed a lease for an apartment, Frank got hired by a tree company in Santa Barbara, and I found a yoga studio where I would teach meditation and a spa to offer reflexology. Everything had fallen into place easily. We spent the rest of our time vacationing in Santa Monica. Frank returned to Pittsburgh on Sunday, September 10th. He was excited to wrap up his old life and ready to start a new chapter within a month in California.

28

The fifth week of my journey started with clear skies and sunshine. Early morning I took a stroll to Santa Monica's Palisades Park. I looked out over the pier, the Pacific Coast Highway and the ocean. Wind shuffled through my hair and I tied it into a ponytail. Behind me traffic backed up on Ocean Avenue. Car horns beeped. People rushed in a hectic pace while the homeless crawled out of their sleeping bags.

The glistening light created the illusion of a silver lining above the turquoise ocean. I focused my gaze at a distant point on the horizon. Every cell in my body relaxed. Thankfully I acknowledged that everything I had wished for had manifested easily.

I continued my walk along tall palm trees and then returned to the hotel. I loaded the bike, checked out, and traveled east. My hands that had defined themselves by caressing the skin of the man I loved for the past week now tightly fit into protective leather gloves and firmly gripped the handlebars. The machine purred reliably. Maintaining the relaxed state that I had established earlier at the ocean, I zoomed through traffic on Highway 10.

Hours later, I crossed the Colorado River into Arizona. Burned ochre dominated the bone dry land and the sculpted sandstone formations. Saguaro cactuses watched silently. I rode through purgatory heat and meditated to stay calm. I thought of Frank and my heart opened. A gentle trickle of love permeated me. I kept on focusing on our happy moments together and the trickle turned into a stream. I felt a sense of lust, longing and the excitement of being in love. The lust turned into a desire to be in love with my life. It was easy to accomplish while traveling and seeking new adventures everyday. Yes, I felt an orgasmic sense of ecstasy on this trip. 'This is how being alive should feel like,' I thought. I desired tasting the rich, luscious life to its fullest.

I meditated on Frank, on my life, and now the love extended to all people I felt connected to, from the past, the present and the future. The stream of love grew into an ocean. I was carried away until I caught myself yet again going faster than I was allowed. Carefully my right foot tapped the rear brake, and I adjusted to the permitted speed.

Late afternoon I completed a 426-mile journey and pulled up to a house in a nice Scottsdale neighborhood. The garage door opened automatically. My friend Isabel had seen me arrive and welcomed me with a big smile. I parked my bike next to her husband's BMW GS 1200. Isabel and I had met during a Systemic Family Constellation Training at the Hellinger Institute in Washington, DC. Since then, her husband, Carlos, had accepted a position as an architect in Scottsdale, and the family had moved to Arizona.

Isabel wore cherry colored pants, a blouse and a pearl necklace. She was tall and slender. Long dark hair fell softly to her shoulders; her hazel eyes radiated warmth. Born to a Venezuelan father and an Austrian mother, Isabel spoke fluent German, Spanish, French and English. Our deep inner transformation work that we shared during our training in DC had created a strong bond. I loved Isabel's introspective sensitivity. To me it felt as if she were surrounded by an aura of quiet classical music.

We unloaded the bike and carried my luggage to the guest room. The house was spacious, open and filled with light. The back door offered a view to the courtyard, a pool, a hot tub and a green oasis of hibiscus, palms, a ficus tree and blossoming orange and purple lantanas.

"After dinner we can relax in the pool," Isabel suggested. "We'll have to pick up Marina from a play date in a little bit. Do you want to take a shower first and freshen up?"

Quickly I rinsed off and put on fresh clothes that weren't soaked in sweat. Then we drove across Scottsdale to pick up Marina, Isabel's nine-year-old daughter. Marina looked like her mom with long dark hair and beautiful eyes; her movements were fluid and confident, her face just a tad rounder, like her dad's. Marina seemed mature for her age. She was outgoing, always gazing straight into a person's eyes, curious about how they would reveal themselves to her. She greeted me in English and switched to Spanish when she spoke to her mom.

Back at the house, we prepared dinner, and Carlos, also a motorcycle enthusiast, arrived from work. Our conversation revolved around bikes, road trips and Isabel's frustration of feeling left out when Carlos took off with his friends on the weekends to go riding.

"I'll get a motorcycle license when Marina is older; then we can go for rides together," Isabel said.

"Mom, why not now?" Marina begged. Isabel affectionately stroked her daughter's hair.

"You have to grow taller, maybe when you are 12 or 13." Isabel said.

"Yes, and then we'll get Mommy a nice Ducati 1198," Carlos suggested.

Isabel and I laughed. Carlos didn't hide how much he wanted the Ducati for himself. "We'll see," Isabel concluded.

Tuesday, September 12th. We drove to the Franciscan Renewal Center in Scottsdale. The Casa Labyrinth, a 7-circuit classical pattern laid out in river rock, was at the back of the spiritual oasis' white buildings, facing scorched hills. The air felt rich with energy. We prepared ourselves for the walk standing in the meager shade of a Palo Verde tree. Isabel had walked the labyrinth before but was interested in receiving proper instructions.

"There is no wrong way to approach a labyrinth. Simply surrender to its mystery and trust the unknown," I said.

We were silent for a moment, and then Isabel spoke. "I feel the presence of my sister. Sofia is right here with me." She pointed to the empty space to her left. Her sister had died in October of 2005. "I'll walk the labyrinth in honor of her life."

Isabel embarked first, and I waited until the impulse emerged to join. I took one step into the labyrinth's field and instantly connected to my dad. His sudden death had left a void and many unanswered questions. I had not had the chance to say goodbye. He died two days after my mom's birthday, on May 15, 1998. I had flown to Germany for the funeral and then returned to the States. My mom and I talked on the phone every day, and she reported a peculiar occurrence. Before he died, my dad had picked roses for her from the rose garden. However, the bouquet of red roses wouldn't die. They lived on for five weeks until they finally wilted.

I journeyed through the twists and turns and recalled memories of my dad. We were bonded by our love for horses, a passion that he had instilled in me. We rode on fox hunts and in the parades of the village celebrations. He taught me how to milk cows, which I was eager to learn as a child. Later as a teenager I sometimes dreaded the farm work. We also shared a ritual on the second morning of Christmas. While my mom cooked, we would close ourselves in the dining room and he would tell me about the war.

As a young girl, having seen the footage on TV, I thought the world must have been in black and white only. I asked my dad how it felt to live in a black and white world. He didn't understand my question, and when I explained that war was bad and in a bad world there were no colors, he shook his head. I didn't realize that during a war the sky was blue.

Isabel passed me in silence; she was on her way out just as I reached the labyrinth's center. I felt surrounded by a strong invisible force that made the hair on my neck stand up.

Instantaneously, I was catapulted back to our farm close to the River Rhine in Germany. I saw myself as a young girl, maybe eleven or twelve. My hair was blonde and very short. It was Christmas time. Dressed in a white blouse, red sweater and grey woolen trousers, I sat next to my father in the dining room. It was nice to see his younger self. His hair was still black and full and his face was clean shaven. He didn't have a beard then. He wore dark brown dress pants and a white button-up shirt. With his big callused farmer's hands he loosened his tie. We must have just returned from church. A red candle flickered in the middle of the table, surrounded by a wreath of fir branches. Their scent filled the room with a fresh crispness. The lights were turned on. Outside it was grey, wet and foggy and even the large windows didn't allow for enough daylight to come in. All furniture was heavy and made of solid oak. The wallpaper displayed hunting scenes, showing dogs, deer and horsemen. I heard my mom in the kitchen, cooking, and assumed my brother was in the living room watching TV.

My dad shared memories from his youth.

The door opened and my mom entered to get a porcelain dish from the cupboard. She wore a red dress and a starched white apron. She touched my dad's shoulder and then looked at me. "I don't know why you need to hear all those stories about World War II. Let the past be the past." She didn't wait for a response. "Lunch is ready soon," she said and then closed the door behind her.

My dad continued, "My older cousin Hans was engaged to a Jewish woman. He was a teacher in Düsseldorf and when the Nazis came to power they threatened that he would lose his job if he married his Jewish fiancé. He began planning her escape to Holland. Then one night they paddled in a rubber dinghy from Düsseldorf to the farm, halfway to safety. They hid out here for one day, and at night, as soon as it was dark enough, they continued to Holland."

"So she was out of danger?" I asked.

"No, not at all. I don't think so." My dad shook his head and looked down at his hands.

"Soon after the Germans invaded Holland and Hans lost contact with his fiancée. He had planned for her to hide out for as long as needed and until it was safe to return to Germany.

Nobody saw a world war coming. After the war ended he searched for her, but years had passed and he never found a trace. She didn't have a lot of money and Hans couldn't imagine that she had gotten away." My dad paused. I sat still. Then he went on and I listened. "Those were horrendous times. And you couldn't trust anyone. No one. The day after her escape to Holland, my cousin went back to work in Düsseldorf so that he wouldn't evoke suspicion. My parents hammered into my mind to keep the secret and not to tell anyone. They knew if someone found out the whole family would be shot and killed."

"Dad, how old were you then?"

"Ten, younger than you are now," he said. "Well, I kept on going to school like everything was normal and also built trenches with the Hitler Youth. I never said a word. I knew we would all get killed." My dad stopped, he put both of his hands, palms down, flat on the table in front of him. "You know I saw her only once, Hans' fiancée," he said. "My parents were very strict and cautious and they didn't want me around. But I saw her coming out of the cellar at night, before they continued in the dinghy to Holland. She was tall and pretty. And I will never forget her eyes. She had the most beautiful blue eyes. She looked right at me until my mother hushed me away. I always remembered her eyes. I wish she had survived, but we'll never know."

I stepped out of the labyrinth's center and felt sad. My mind was spinning with questions about the Jewish fiancée. How did she feel when she was left by herself in Holland? What happened to her? I tried to broaden my perspective to all those who went missing. There were so many. The subject was far too big for me to meditate upon. Tears came to my eyes. Then I took a few deep breaths and bowed to the forces of the universe that I didn't understand. Slowly I moved on and became aware again of my surroundings, the dry hills and the resilient bushes that survived in the desert.

Then I followed a walkway to the meditation chapel where I met up with Isabel. The space was quiet and soothing. Light filtered into primary colors through artful stained glass windows. We shared our experiences and some time later we left the sanctuary.

The next two days, I stayed with Isabel, Carlos and Marina. Every evening we enjoyed a swim in the pool and a relaxing soak in the hot tub. On Thursday morning, September 14th, Carlos swung into the saddle of his Beemer, wearing a protective jacket over his business suit. He accompanied me for a few miles on Frank Lloyd Wright Boulevard. At the junction of Shea Boulevard, he turned right. We waved to each other, and then I continued left toward scenic road 87, heading to Sedona.

29

The burned-out land turned green. I climbed higher into pine forested mountains and clear skies showed dark bruises. Then the wind picked up, shrieked inside my helmet and I stopped to put on rain gear. Precisely the moment I zipped up my protection; fat drops of rain began pounding. I rode 200 miles in tough weather and arrived in Sedona, just as sunrays dared to peek again through the clouds. The spectacular landscape of red rock monoliths appeared animated in the rapidly changing play of light and shadow.

I pulled up next to four Harley Davidson motorcycles parked in front of the tourist information center. Wet stairs led up to the entrance. The office was packed with people, and I squeezed myself through the crowd to the information flyers. A woman spoke German. I turned my head. She was dressed in biker leathers. A tall bald man wore the same outfit. They talked to three other couples, all in their fifties, leafing through the flyers while figuring out which sights to visit.

"Those Harleys out there are yours?" I said in German.

"Yes," she said. "You are out on a bike, too?

"Yes," I nodded. It was obvious; I was still in my rain gear and carried my helmet and tank bag.

"By yourself?" Another woman said. Now they all turned toward me.

"Yes, going cross country for six weeks." Three out of the four women frowned.

"Where are you from in Germany?" I continued, ignoring the facial expressions, "It's always nice to meet fellow Germans."

"From the Düsseldorf area."

"That is where I am from, but I live in the U.S. now." Since they weren't warming up to me I just kept talking. "Looks like you are on a nice trip, too. Where are you going?"

"Well, we flew into L.A.," a man responded. "We're doing a guided motorcycle tour for three weeks. We went through California, now Arizona and then on to New Mexico and Colorado. The organizer has booked the hotels and carries our luggage in a van; we meet up with him every evening."

"So during the day you are free to do your own thing?" I asked.

"Yes. We got maps and travel suggestions, and we are independent during the day."

"What a great way to travel. That's awesome," I said.

"It's a trip of a lifetime," the woman I talked to first chimed in. "We planned this trip for three whole years."

"And we need to enjoy every moment," her husband continued. "A journey like this will never happen again." He was seriously determined and didn't smile.

"Why not? If you have a great time, why wouldn't you do it again?" I was baffled.

A tall man with thinning hair and a bushy grey mustache looked at me and shook his head. "You can only go once in your life on a trip of a lifetime." He raised his chin and then exclaimed, "So you are traveling all alone."

"Yes," I said and went on to share my itinerary, mentioning labyrinths.

"Labyrinths? What are labyrinths? Never heard of them," he shook his head again, then paused and looked at his friends, but they all shrugged their shoulders. I showed the picture on my tank bag and briefly explained that I was on a spiritual journey.

"Now I see why you are traveling by yourself. That would not be for everybody," he said and shook his head a third time. Politely we wished each other safe travels, and I turned to the information desk.

I picked up a map of the famous energy vortexes and a brochure for the Angel Valley Spiritual Center. A secluded, peaceful sanctuary surrounded by the Coconino National Forest sounded like the perfect place to stay.

A 20 minute drive west of Sedona brought me to a gravel dirt road. Wet from the rain, the surface felt slippery, and I steered the heavily loaded bike at crawling speed. The road wound along hillsides and from the highest point I overlooked the peaceful valley, a green haven including a tipi village, a labyrinth, a medicine wheel and wooden guest houses along Oak Creek. I took a few deep breaths to fill my being with the beauty of this place, realizing that I would not be able to stay. There was no restaurant and I had to go back into town for dinner. The two-mile dirt road was too difficult to navigate at night or in the rain. I decided to find lodging in Sedona, but first I opted to walk the labyrinth.

The classical 7-circuit pattern was laid out in river rock. The center circle contained larger sand-colored boulders that offered the seeker the comfort of sitting down for introspection. Bushes and white flowering shrubs surrounded the labyrinth. Emerald hills formed a protective circle around the property. Red rugged layers of rock burst naked out of the serenity of green.

I walked around the labyrinth in a clockwise direction. The issue for this walk was easy to find. The conversation with the Germans was still stirring within me. I understood their way of thinking, the need to categorize and to see life unfold in an orderly fashion. I am German, too. For the couples from Düsseldorf, it was a fact that a trip of a lifetime could not be repeated once it was done. Why did they feel limited to go on only one big adventure in their life? Who made the rules and why did they accept such limitations? To me it seemed that they were financially able to afford more than one big trip. But who knew? If anything, I was to blame for making assumptions. I projected my own feelings and the memories about my quarrels with my parents into this encounter.

But then still, the rebel voice within me said, 'I am on a trip of a lifetime, too. And I will do another trip of a lifetime, then another and then another. My journey of growth will continue indefinitely.'

So here I was in this heavenly place and not at peace at all. The Germans reflected something deep within me that I didn't want to look at. Otherwise, it wouldn't have bothered me. A flexible person cannot be bent out of shape. I clearly wasn't as flexible as I wished to be.

I took a deep breath and moved into the sacred circle. The first steps brought a new state of consciousness. My mind went blank, as if someone had turned a switch and instantly all previous thoughts evaporated. A burden lifted. 'This is good,' I thought and turned deeper into the labyrinth. It felt as if I were floating in an ocean of light. Then I reached the center, sat down on a rock and closed my eyes. I asked what I needed to learn from this experience.

An image appeared inside my head. I saw a black box filled with darkness. Infinite, benevolent light engulfed the box. The box was the only black spot in a light-filled universe. Inside this box, millions of people were trapped, tapping in the dark. They felt separated from one another and suffered enormous pain, completely unaware that the light was all around.

I realized that the labyrinth invited me to step out of judgment and into unity. At the core, I was one with all humanity and all of creation. I needed to seek what connected us and not what separated us. Essentially we all wanted the same: to be loved, to feel love and to live in peace. So what if people only went on one trip of a lifetime? Wasn't life a continuous journey of growth and learning wherever we were? Did it matter if we traveled or stayed at home? And so what if I was German, Catholic, and maybe Jewish? Or if my skin color was white, black, yellow or red? All of these were just identifications. None of it mattered.

I recalled my teacher Gilad's words when I first learned to meditate. He had explained that by shining light into darkness, the darkness turns into light. He had also said that the light is all around, but to find it, we need to look inside our hearts. We can go through life and search in all the wrong places. But one day we'll look within and we'll find the entire universe.

Gratefully, I acknowledged that this labyrinth experience mended my separated way of thinking back to wholeness and reminded me of who I really am.

I returned to my bike and before putting on my helmet, I looked up into the sky. Voluptuous, white clouds chased above. At higher altitudes the wind drew brushstrokes of silver. Then my gaze turned to the puddle of muddy water next to the bike. The spectacle of the heavens reflected on its surface, revealing a swirling tango of light and shadow. Smiling I got back on my machine and started the engine. Nervous movement hushed through the underbrush and a small animal darted out. A hare sped off across the dirt road, its oversized ears flapped like huge spoons. My mouth dropped open, and then it occurred to me that the curious creature was a jack rabbit. Not a cartoon character or a mystical invention, it was a real animal and this was my first time seeing one.

I was stunned and marveled at the variety of nature as I carefully navigated the dirt road. The encounter with the Germans and the insights during my labyrinth walk made me realize that I had to continually observe my thoughts and not get trapped by my own judgments. Life is large, if I allowed it to be. I felt thankful to have learned another lesson. Then I reached the asphalted main road, opened the throttle and headed back into town.

30

I inquired at four different hotels, all of them booked, until I found a room for three nights at the Sedona Real Inn. Two handsome men in their forties, John and Chuck from Philadelphia, engaged me in conversation. They were excited to hear about my adventure and asked detailed questions about labyrinths and their meaning.

"That is very courageous and so cool. Can we take pictures with you and your motorcycle?" John asked.

Touched by the men's enthusiasm and the contrast to my earlier conversation with the Germans, I agreed to a brief photo session. Then I parked the bike close to the room, unloaded the luggage, took a quick shower and looked at my labyrinth walk invitation.

Judy Massey, a retired French teacher, had served as a translator for Dr. Lauren Artress at the Chartres Cathedral in France. She had translated the lectures of Father Francois Legaux, the cathedral's rector at the time. Judy organized labyrinth events in Sedona. She had responded to my message through the facilitator network and invited me to the St. Andrews's Episcopal Church on 100 Arroyo Pinon Drive. My hotel was conveniently located on 95 Arroyo Pinon Drive.

'The mysterious ways of the universe have brought me to the right place,' I thought, reflecting upon my arduous hotel search. Instead of getting into my armor of biker gear and sturdy boots, I slipped into light cotton pants, a T-shirt and sandals.

A short walk across the street brought me to the church's parking lot, which was closed off with yellow tape. Bright blue colors marked an 11-circuit Chartres replica on black asphalt, measuring roughly 50 feet. The church, a modern building with a natural stone façade, displayed an artistic cross next to the front entrance.

I entered through the wide open doors. Judy Massey, a petite, energetic, blonde woman in her early sixties arranged information brochures and labyrinth books on a table. Several people sat in quiet contemplation in the creative area, coloring labyrinth patterns with crayons and water colors. Soft music played from a CD player. I introduced myself and Judy's face lit up into a bright smile. Her blue eyes sparkled.

"Welcome, it is so wonderful that you could make it," she said and hugged me. Judy was not at all surprised to hear how I had found the hotel close to the labyrinth.

"You were already connected to its field; it guided you here. Synchronicities are rampant around labyrinths," she said. "The first thing Lauren would ask students arriving in Chartres was if there had been any unusual encounters and synchronicities that had guided them to France. Everyone had raised their hands and had stories to tell. It seems that everything is orchestrated by a higher force which guides us in a perfectly divine way. And it's a universal phenomenon with labyrinths."

I noted that it was interesting to find a labyrinth in the parking lot, not the common sacred area. Judy laughed. "We didn't have much space, only one big parking lot. So I came up with the idea to paint on the asphalt. I'll show you how we did it." She signaled me to follow her, as she whizzed outside.

The wind had picked up and a row of 40-foot tall larch trees waved elegantly, swaying back and forth. We arrived at the labyrinth. Judy stopped and opened her arms wide, as if embracing the circle.

"We used blue highway paint. My son and I invented the sponge mop technique. We marked the outline with chalk, but we didn't want to be on our knees. It also would have been difficult to make perfectly round lines. The sponge mop creates the effect of brick shapes."

"That's genius. I would never have guessed this is a sponge mop pattern," I said, examining the blue shapes, each one unique and artistic.

"It is very cost-effective, too," Judy added.

I closed my eyes and tuned into the labyrinth's energy field. A gentle hum surrounded me and I sensed the vibration of the light. My body relaxed, my breathing slowed, and I felt as if a clear mountain stream rushed through me. "It is very powerful," I said. Images flashed in front of my inner eye and I shared the emerging vision with Judy.

Six years ago my friend Dr. Sue Gaulden, a math professor, had asked me to teach meditation to inner city teenagers in Newark, New Jersey. Sue directed a summer program called Project G.R.A.D. (Graduating Really Achieves Dreams). The program was designed to create academic enrichment, but it also kept the kids off the streets and out of trouble. Forty percent of the 14- and 15-year-old African American teens didn't live with their parents. The teenagers grew up in an environment of drug addiction, violence and teen pregnancy.

I had chosen to introduce the group to the tree meditation. First we stood in a circle, holding hands and the group of thirty teens visualized themselves as strong and healthy trees, connecting to their inner source of strength and wisdom. The second part of the meditation took place in a lying position. The group got comfortable on mats and blankets. I played quartz crystal singing bowls, a tool for sound-healing, which induces alpha wave level activity of the brain, a relaxed state of mind. Then I guided the group with a soothing voice through a progressive relaxation technique and a nature walk to connect with their own personal tree. The teenagers were exceptionally receptive to meditation. The boys, who had been the loudest and the center of attention, fell asleep during the second meditation. Everyone reported deep states of relaxation. A girl who suffered from a headache at the beginning of the class was surprised that her pain was gone.

The teenagers' lives had been deprived in so many ways, and there was a real need to fill their lack of safety and stability. Sue and I had discussed continuing a meditation program at the school. When I taught at the University of Pittsburgh Medical Center, my courses were continually evaluated. Students, who had completed 10-week courses, reported life changing positive benefits, including improved sleep, decreased pain, improved concentration and energy level, decreased anxiety and improved well-being and ability to cope with stress. Sue and I had felt that a meditation program would change these young peoples' lives and ensure a better future. But there was no funding available. So much good work could be done, but without proper guidance the teens would easily fall back into their old thought patterns and the influence of a destructive environment.

The vision of a cost-effective labyrinth pattern took shape. The teenagers could paint a sacred circle in their schoolyard. It could be integrated as an art project or be part of religious studies or even math as an exploration of sacred geometry. A permanent labyrinth would offer tremendous benefit to students.

"It's a great idea to create labyrinths in disadvantaged neighborhoods," Judy agreed.

"Yes. And the pattern itself creates a positive energy field that affects its environment. To me it looks like a tower of swirling light. So even if it appears two-dimensional it creates a three-dimensional space," I added.

"Not only that. There is more to it," Judy continued. "Labyrinths are sprouting up everywhere. I receive invitations for labyrinth dedications at least twice a month. It's mind-boggling. The labyrinth patterns connect an energetic grid around the earth. Like acupuncture points on the body. They create a matrix of higher consciousness."

"Have you heard of Toby Evans?" I asked, and Judy shook her head. I went on to tell her about my visit at Toby's Prairie Labyrinth near Kansas City and the Art Line Project that aimed to create labyrinths along the 39th latitude, the heart line of America. The Art Line reactivates an old ley line and connects natural energy vortex points to sacred sites, also channeling light into Washington, DC.

"That's very fascinating. I'll have to look into it," Judy said. "One of the first times I went with Lauren to Chartres she made a profound comment while we were sitting at the breakfast table. She peppered her egg and then paused and as if struck by inspiration. She said, 'We need to pepper the planet with labyrinths.' Look where we are now, eighteen years later. Labyrinths have inspired a worldwide movement toward peace, love and harmony."

People started arriving for the labyrinth walk. Judy introduced me to her friends. Then she pushed the play button on her tape player, and we listened to melodious flute music. She invited us to walk the labyrinth. I entered last. In unison our group of 15 people circled deeper into the mysterious web.

Crickets chirped. Their song traveled from the creek behind the church, grew in intensity and then overpowered the flute music. I felt comforted by the presence of larch trees. A wave of familiarity and belonging filled my heart, reminding me of the larches on our farm in Germany. My gaze went up along the slender tree branches to the delicate light green needles and into the heavens. A spectacle in deep indigo, purple and lilac brewed into a storm. The dark blue center focused like an eye in the sky. Oblivious the seekers followed their path looking down, everyone contained in their own little world. Wind caressed my skin then suddenly tugged me with a forceful pull. 'Where to?' I asked.

Thunder cracked and echoed its loud roar from the church building. At once we all stopped and stared up. Flashes of lightning zigzagged through the sky. My heart jumped, began to race.

'A little storm,' I thought. 'No reason to get nervous.' I looked around and saw the fellow labyrinth walkers picking up their pace. A woman whispered, "It is going to rain."

I kept my pace slow and steady, trying not to be influenced by the others. But in the labyrinth, we were all one. In tune with everybody's energy, my body had responded to the sudden shift of group consciousness.

I recalled a research study that had examined how one man's thoughts affect the well-being of another person. Test candidates were assigned to separate rooms in a laboratory. One person was connected to measuring devices monitoring heart rate, blood pressure, brain wave level activity and perspiration. The other person was instructed to send thoughts of friendship, benevolence and peace. The test person had shown an immediate relaxation response, as heart rate, blood pressure and brain wave level activity went down.

Then thoughts of hostility and anger were sent, and instantly all measurements had peaked; the test person had shown an acute stress response.

Every thought that enters our mind creates reality; every thought we think about another person affects them in an either positive or negative way. I focused on seeing myself filled with light and envisioned sending the light to all human beings. When I approached the center, one by one the fellow seekers stepped out of the labyrinth. I was left alone. The wind ceased. I relaxed and continued my solitary journey.

The rain never came.

Following the labyrinth walk, I spent a nice evening by myself, enjoyed dinner, returned to the hotel, wrote in my journal, then watched TV and fell asleep. At night, I awoke out of a dreamless empty space. The alarm clock's red numbers showed the time at 3:33 a.m. I turned around and dozed off quickly. The next day I explored the famous Sedona energy vortexes and at night I awoke again at exactly 3:33 am. The same mystifying phenomena occurred during the third night.

Judy Massey mentioned that people visiting Sedona often couldn't sleep due to the intense spiritual energy charge. I slept well. But still, unknown forces operated on me at night and awakened me with precise accuracy.

31

Three days later I had made the 438-mile trip from Sedona to Santa Fe and was walking the winding path of the Evolution Labyrinth. This excursion focused around a giant metal butterfly that towered on top of a 12-foot wooden totem in the center.

I was in the midst of a lush private garden, surrounded by unbound greenery and flowers blossoming in abundant red, purple, sky blue, orange, magenta and bright yellow. The sweet scent of honeysuckle saturated the air. Bronze sculptures of headless naked ladies graced this untamed abundance. The passing of time had tinted their lush curves to a pale green as delicate layers of the bronze surface peeled. When I turned my head, the light changed and out of the corner of my eye I perceived the eerie illusion of liveliness, as if they were breathing, watching me with neither heads nor eyes to see. The main house was camouflaged underneath layers of wild fern. A sand-colored adobe wall sealed this oasis of art and imagination from the outside world.

The labyrinth was based on the pattern of the Ely Cathedral Labyrinth in Britain. Unlike the ones I had visited before, this was not round but of a square design. The path was marked by metal slats. Eight metal towers along the labyrinth's path depicted evolutionary steps from the first crawling creatures that inhabited the planet to the dinosaurs, the dinosaurs' extinction, ape and then man.

Fine gravel crunched underneath my sandals as I passed the Big Bang, a four-foot tall metal tower, painted with colorful bursting stars showing the birth of our universe. Then followed metal pillars revealing the four elements air, fire, water and earth, colored in dark and sky blue, ochre and fiery reds.

The giant butterfly hovered high above on top of the totem in the labyrinth's center. Thoughts galloped through my mind but eventually settled on the winged creature, the universal symbol for spiritual transformation.

I couldn't get the idea out of my mind that when the caterpillar thinks life is over, it is just the beginning. I recalled the story of a man who found a butterfly's cocoon. Then one day he saw a small opening appear. He watched the butterfly struggle to get its body through the little hole. It appeared that the butterfly was stuck. The man brought a pair of scissors and snipped off the remaining bits of the cocoon. The butterfly emerged easily, but its body was swollen and its wings stayed small and shriveled. It crawled around with a swollen body and shrunken wings, never able to fly. The man had failed to understand that the butterfly needed to struggle through the tiny opening to force the fluids from its body into its wings so that it would be ready for flight once it had achieved its freedom from the cocoon. The struggle was exactly what the butterfly needed.

I reached the labyrinth's center. The totem was a carefully carved piece of woodwork with embedded doors, which opened to an unknown hidden space. I took the two handles, opened the doors and saw my reflection in a mirror. A subtitle read in calligraphic letters, 'What is your responsibility?' I studied my expression and saw in the background the path I had traversed. Then my gaze wandered back to my reflection. I looked into my eyes. For just a brief moment everything shifted, and I felt as if I were looking into my father's eyes. Mine are shaped like his and as I age, I see wrinkles arranging themselves in the exact natural way around the lids and corners of my eyes. Even the color shifted. My dad's eyes had been a piercing green and mine are blue, but sometimes the light played tricks and then they were just like his. "Wow," I said and then my eyes turned blue. The moment had passed.

I read the question aloud, emphasizing every word as if to taste its essence. "What is your responsibility?" I knew that if I lived with the question long enough the answer would come. Then I returned to the beginning.

On September 20th, I crossed from New Mexico through Colorado into Kansas and followed the Arkansas River. A country road took me through forgotten towns. Abandoned motels and out-of-service fuel stations watched time go by as they silently faltered into states of decay. Beyond fields of lush green meadows, the shimmering surface of the quiet river was visible in the distance. I was content with the moment, happy to travel, even though I knew that I was in the homestretch, less than 2,000 miles from Pittsburgh. I could travel ever onward, I thought, never arrive anywhere, just keep on going.

Then butterflies appeared. Lovely, yellow butterflies. I considered them as a sign that I was on the right track, thinking the right thoughts. Then the first butterfly smashed onto my visor, the sound an aching splotch. For a moment I imagined I heard the butterfly scream as its body disintegrated into messy smear and blocked my vision. Then more and more butterflies came, thousands of butterflies, smashing onto my visor, making it impossible to see.

"Holy shit," I said aloud. I hit the brake, and the bike slowed to 50 miles per hour, then 40, then 30. I found myself in the midst of a butterfly inferno.

Completely blinded by what I saw as a symbol for spiritual transformation and rebirth, I considered the irony of this scenario.

I opened the visor; yellow butterflies smashed onto my face. Desperate flapping wings touched my skin. But the butterflies' destiny was sealed. Their salty bitter taste overwhelmed my lips and mouth.

I pulled into the next fuel station. People busily cleaned the windshields of cars while waving away with arms and hands the oncoming storm of butterflies. I walked straight to the bathroom and washed my face and the helmet's visor. Then I asked the woman behind the store counter about the unusual phenomenon.

"It's hatching season. It's only two days every year. But it's messy, eh?" She moved her head up and down, pointing to my jacket and leathers. I was completely covered with dead butterfly carcasses.

"It's not pretty," I nodded.

"Not a good time to be out on a bike," she said.

"I guess," I said, walked back to my machine and waved away the flying creatures. My poor bike was a messy spectacle, too. I wondered how long it would take me to clean off the sun crusted remains. Then I continued to travel, slowly for the next hours, stopping every once in a while, to clean my visor. A futile attempt because soon after countless dead bodies smeared all over again.

Late in the afternoon the bombardment ceased, and I found myself chasing my own shadow on spine straight Kansas roads. Mile after mile I contemplated the meaning of life and my role in it. Seeing my own shadow ahead of me, I realized that if we shine light into the shadow, the shadow turns into light.

Late evening, towering clouds appeared with royal majesty and unleashed a serious downpour. I spent the night in Garden City and by 9:00 a.m. I was back on the road. My bike had been washed clean, but now relentless rain hammered like cannonballs onto my helmet. This rain was not blue, light and cleansing. Not invigorating, bringing out the scents of earth. This rain was dark and heavy. It erased the horizon and the view of lush green Kansas fields. The land around disappeared, as if it never was.

I tried to entertain my mind with spiritual thoughts, contemplated that the outside world was a reflection of the inside world. Consequently, everything I perceived revealed my inner self. 'Was my head in the clouds? Where was the light? Was sunshine a certainty above the clouds? Why couldn't I see the light even though I knew it was there?' I wondered. 'Yes,' I thought, 'our heads are round so that thoughts can change direction. But in this nothingness there was nowhere to go.' The rain increased its fury and despite my mental aerobics, I had to admit that I was putting myself in danger. I was frustrated. I had to get off the road, get out of the rain.

In the next little town I pulled into the parking lot of a restaurant and ran to the entry room. I peeled myself out of my rain gear while taking a quick glance into the main room. All tables were filled and every chair at the bar was taken. The hostess looked surprised and asked, "A table for only one?"

"Yes," I answered. She took me to a single booth next to a table with eleven properly dressed women with perfect make-up and hairdos. I put my rain gear and tank bag onto the floor and puddles of water immediately spread. I wrung out my soaked ponytail and wiped my neck dry with a napkin. The women's conversation had stopped and they stared at me.

I smiled, trying to be polite to the impolite faces. Soon their chit chat resumed.

I ordered lunch and then phoned my mom. She promptly answered.

"Thank God you are there," I said and told her briefly about my last hours.

"Why are you doing this?" my mom asked. "Sometimes I wonder if you are my daughter. You are not afraid of the devil."

My mom always referred to the devil when she criticized how I lived my life.

"Mom, there is no devil, only my own self and the shadows that I deconstruct when I go through these experiences. And it's not always easy."

"I have no idea what you are talking about. You could have stayed at home, like everyone else, married a good man, have two or three kids. Really, I would have loved to have grandchildren. And you could have had a very nice life. Now you are out there by yourself in the rain in a foreign country."

The ideal life that my mom envisioned didn't exist for me. I looked around and suddenly felt friendlier toward the women at the nearby table, the way they looked at me and talked quietly behind their hands. Or the old man behind the newspaper, who occasionally lifted his head and scrutinized me with furrowed brows. And the young couple at the table next to me, who seemed to be listening to my conversation. Maybe they were just trying to figure out which language I spoke.

I was the stranger, entering their world. This was not different from my own hometown, where everybody knew everybody and everybody had their noses in each other's business. Maybe that's why I felt agitated when I first sat down, because I knew this small town environment so well.

'But then,' I thought, 'we were all just living our lives.' I felt sure that the people around me had questions, too. Also wondered sometimes where we came from, where we are going and what life is all about. It's part of human nature.

My mom continued to rant about how she always had to worry about me, when I went backpacking in Brazil, when I lived in Israel with the terrorism and during Desert Storm and now this. But eventually she got tired of it, as always, and we had a pleasant conversation. Every few days I sent her postcards and many had already arrived. She asked questions about the places I had seen and I was happy that she was there. It was all I needed. We continued to talk throughout my meal until the waitress cleaned the table and then we said goodbye.

At the restaurant's entry room, I put on my rain gear and helmet. People were turning their heads, surely wondering who this crazy person could be. I didn't care. I chose my experiences, and I owned them, for better or for worse. The thought of taking a hotel room and surrendering to the weather was inconceivable.

I pulled back into traffic, my visor half open so that it wouldn't fog up. Rain lashed onto my face and I exclaimed, "Rain, you cannot conquer me. Bless the hardship. Bless the struggle. Bless the rain."

This positive state of mind stayed with me until I merged into traffic on I-70 going east. Eighteen-wheelers blasted by at eighty miles per hour, splashing up fountains of water that brought my vision down to zero. Fierce side winds swept over the plains, took me by surprise and nearly threw me into the other lane. I rode slowly, 50 miles per hour. At higher speeds I would have risked losing control. My fists grabbed the handlebars and held firmly against unpredictable blows of wind.

Then, when I thought it couldn't get much worse, the seam of my rain gear burst open, torn by the wind. Weatherproof fabric flapped like a broken wing. A gaping hole over my right shoulder made me feel vulnerable. The intimate purr of my machine, which always soothed my nerves, had long been overpowered by the hammering sound of rain on my helmet. But now the tattered rain gear created a violent hissing. Exhausted I pulled into the next fuel station, took a break and warmed up with a cup of hot chocolate. Then I rode on. The weather never eased.

I concluded a tough day and 419.4 miles in heavy rain at an Irish pub near Kansas City. I listened to eighties music, ate Shepherd's Pie and drank beer. When I got ready to leave a familiar song started playing. "You can't always get what you want. But if you try sometimes, well you just might find, you get what you need." I smiled, thought of Erin and ran through the rain back to my hotel.

Later in bed, I wished I could snuggle up next to Frank and sleep for 24 hours. When I tried to call him, he didn't answer and his mailbox was full.

32

The next morning came early at 7:00 a.m. Rain drummed against the window. I opened the curtains and looked at dark grey skies, then went back to bed and phoned my mom.

"Frank has been unreachable the last days," I complained.

"Out of sight, out of mind," my mom answered.

"Yes, I know," I said.

We chatted a little longer and then I asked if I could call the next day at the same time. It was 1:00 p.m. in Germany.

"Sure, I will be here."

"Thank you, mom." I knew I could count on her. "Well, I'd better start my day. I hope it clears up. I am tired of riding in the rain."

"Please, be careful," she said.

"Always."

One hour later I continued to ride east. The rain pounded down on me. Big trucks zoomed by; their loud diesel engines pumped furiously as they hauled their large freights. Fat tires that so easily could crush my bike spewed waves of water at me. I tried hard to stay positive. All my mind could come up with was my mom's favorite saying: When angels travel, the sun shines. 'Where did I go wrong,' I thought.

I had looked forward to returning to Toby's prairie grass labyrinth a second time. The first walk had brought a profound spiritual experience, and as my trip was nearly over it felt important to revisit the sacred circle for a final conclusion. But considering the weather, my chances were slim. I expected to ride in the rain for the rest of the trip, and my impending sense of misery increased. My world had turned grey and heavy. My torn rain gear flapped and hissed like snakes on Medusa's head. Rain soaked my right shoulder and dripped onto my back. I was uncomfortable but rode on.

Several miles before the Blue Springs exit, the sky opened and rays of sun broke out of the clouds. Would I be able to walk Toby's labyrinth? I pulled off the interstate. My excitement grew as I followed the country road. The land was dry as if never touched by the rain. And then I felt the familiar 'click' in my nervous system as if my energy field had locked into the labyrinth's field and began communicating. I felt a tingling sensation rushing up and down my spine. The phenomenon had baffled me the first time, but this time I felt a sense of coming home.

The farm was deserted. Toby had traveled to France to attend a Mary Magdalene Pilgrimage, and her husband was in Kansas City, teaching. I parked the bike next to the apple trees and walked past the art studio to the prairie grass labyrinth.

Golden rods stood in full bloom. The labyrinth was transformed, looked like an ocean of gold waving in the wind. I circled barefoot through the field of bright yellow golden light. This was my easiest walk yet. I didn't think or analyze, just felt one with the energy that pulsed up and down my spine growing stronger than ever before. My whole body tingled; I saw sparks of light dancing in the air, and I heard the sound of the light, a high pitched hum. The scent of ripe prairie grass ready to be harvested filled my nostrils. The warm morning sun caressed my skin. Then I skipped back to the bike and continued my journey.

A couple of hours later I stopped for lunch and checked my messages. One was a voicemail from Frank saying that he had forgotten the phone in his sister's car and that he hadn't been able to call. I didn't feel like calling him back.

Then it rained again. I continued to ride for the rest of the day in bad weather. The next morning also welcomed me with heavy rain. Just as I crossed into Ohio, the clouds dissolved and by the time I reached Columbus the sun triumphed over the sky. I stopped to take off my rain gear and fueled up one last time.

Late afternoon on September 23rd 2006, I rode on familiar Pennsylvania roads. My journey that had started 41 days ago concluded with clear skies, sunshine and thousands of golden fall leaves gliding weightlessly through the air. My machine purred and my heart felt light. I opened the throttle for a few miles and dared not to care about the required speed limit. I loved riding my bike. This was bliss.

An hour later I pulled back into the garage. Frank, who must have heard me arrive, ran toward me. We hugged and kissed and I inhaled his delicious manly scent. "You did it. You did your trip," he said. "How many miles?"

I checked the odometer. "7,430 miles."

"Good job."

We unloaded the bike and Frank carried the heavy luggage. I pressed a button and the garage door automatically closed with a deep baritone thud. My journey was over; my gypsy life ended here, and suddenly, I was overcome with sadness. I followed Frank up the stairs into the house. He looked at me and asked, "What's wrong?"

"It's over and I don't feel like I imagined I would feel: proud, ecstatic or happy. Nothing like that at all. I feel totally empty. I want more."

Frank drew me close, stroked my hair and kissed my forehead. "No worries. In two weeks we'll pack the moving truck and you will be on the road again. Only two weeks. Why don't you relax and I'll cook us dinner."

I showered, then went outside onto the deck and watched the sun set. The sky turned orange. Birds sang. The clear water of the bright turquoise swimming pool shimmered peacefully. Planters on the wooden deck overflowed with crimson, white and purple petunias.

Later in bed, I folded myself into Frank's arms and fell into a long, deep and dreamless sleep.

33

Frank and I arrived in California on October 10, 2006. We were excited about starting a new life together. With the cross-country road trip in my rearview mirror, my life needed a new vision. I was fully focused on building my business.

In our free time, Frank and I went on motorcycle rides. The twelfth day after our arrival we traveled on Highway 101 along the Pacific Coast. My visor was half open. The delicious scent of the sea filled my nostrils. The play of light on the waves, the silver, the aquamarine and the emerald blue enchanted me. I was in the moment. If any doubt about starting a new life together with Frank in California had ever entered my mind, it vanished then.

We turned inland onto the mountainous serpentines of 150, a windy two-lane road. I leaned into the curves, opened the throttle on the straight stretches and slowed again for the turns. Lake Casitas shone like an iridescent jewel of turquoise embraced by the ochre mountains. We turned right toward the ocean. Frank sped off on his silver Yamaha FZ1. At a slower pace, I assessed my life to the perfect hum of my machine while taking in the landscape. At a stop sign, I came to a standstill and then slowly opened the throttle to turn left. Old trees shaded the road. I accelerated and quickly gained speed. I didn't see the sharp left curve ahead. It was too late. No time to brake. Instead of leaning close to the center line, I tried to ride out a larger turn. I hit the gravel and lost control. Time stopped and my bike slithered in slow motion. The next thing I remember was being catapulted through the air; I must have jumped off. I had no concept of time. There was absolute silence. I was thrown sideways, and my view focused like a tunnel vision on my bike. The machine slowly crashed into the guard rail, the front tire buried beneath the rail. The broken turn signals dangled hopelessly by their wire. Slowly the engine cracked open and black oil gushed out.

Then I crashed onto the gravel; the full impact hit my right shoulder, and I heard a snap. Instantly, my perception of time returned to normal. Excruciating pain shot through me. Moments later a green van stopped. A husband and wife jumped out, dialing for help on their cell phone. I tried to sit up in vain, telling myself that everything was okay. Frank rushed to me, his face dark with distress. Carefully he lifted me up, cradled me in his arms. I closed my eyes and drifted off to a calm place without pain.

"Open your eyes. Dorit, don't pass out. Open your eyes." Frank's voice urged me to come back. He was worried. The pain increased and I closed my eyes again. This time I drifted off further. I felt like being pulled upward. A vacuum sucked me in, and at the same time there was no gravity. I realized that I was out of my body, weightless and free. White light protectively wrapped itself around me. I felt safe and I got the sense that there was absolutely nothing that had to be done. It was all right to go, to go even further. Easily I followed the invitation.

Someone called me from afar and I felt forced to turn around.

"Dorit, open your eyes." Frank's voice sounded desperate. I came back into my body, looked into his eyes. I tried to smile but then felt the pain. My eyes closed, and I floated off. This time faster than before, I reached the space of infinite peace. I was surrounded by white light. There was no connection to the physical realm, unlike my out-of-body experiences in deep meditative states, where I would look down on my body and still perceive a physical reality. This was very different and exactly where I wanted to be. Everything was in place; there was nothing left to do.

Frank called my name. I came back, opened my eyes for one moment, closed my eyes and immediately drifted off at light speed, far away from my life on earth. This happened six or seven times.

Frank called me back again and again. Each time his voice sounded farther away, like a distant echo.

But then, suddenly, I was back in my body. A commotion stirred around us. More cars stopped. People rushed toward the accident scene. The fire truck arrived, then the police and finally the ambulance. I was taken to the hospital. X-rays showed no broken bones. The doctor explained that torn muscles, bruises and severe soft tissue damage could be more painful than a broken shoulder. I needed to rest.

The crash clearly warned me not to push forward but to take time to heal and reflect. Every day I went for long walks along the beach, spent hours listening to ocean waves. I watched pelicans dive into the ocean catching fish. Seagulls flew low above the waves, screeching loudly. Sandpipers probed their long beaks into the sand picking food. They nervously rushed away when I came closer. Cool water whirled around my ankles while my feet sank into the wet sand. Inland, the Ventura hills were covered with a slight touch of green, like gentle layers of silk. The two trees, a significant landmark, stood lonely on a distant hill. I enjoyed watching the changing light; bright sun shimmered silver on the ocean, later turning into orange and then disappearing into the Pacific.

With every day that went by something changed within me. The shoulder pain lessened. I noticed a slow surrender to just be, to let life happen to me and not to make big plans for the future. Nothing needed to be done. There was a sense of peace that I couldn't quite grasp yet.

I was experiencing a pivotal shift much like at age 15 when Silke died. 'Had I found the answers to questions about life and death that had catapulted me on a spiritual search for the last two decades?' I wondered. 'And wasn't it ironic that I went all the way across the country and then one moment of carelessness brought the answer?'

I felt grateful to be alive and was amazed that even though I had not been severely injured, I had left my body completely. I knew with certainty that consciousness exists separately from the physical body. A window to a new world had opened. And maybe it wasn't something new, but something familiar, a place my soul knew.

Just like the center of the labyrinth, the place of our origin and our final destination. A place that I had learned to sense labyrinth walk after labyrinth walk after labyrinth walk. 'Funny,' I thought, 'that as humans we aren't afraid of the place from where we came before we were born but are afraid of where we go after dying. And maybe we can only define life if we consciously look at our mortality and view death as a friend, the constant companion on our journey through life.'

Every labyrinth walk had allowed me to grow spiritually, had reminded me who I really am. And maybe this recent out-of-body experience resembled my final transition, which one day for sure will come for me and for everyone of us. And maybe one day we will all meet in this place of pure bliss, peace and infinite light where absolutely nothing needs to be done. One day we will know.

During my time of healing and reflection, I also learned that the site of my crash was called 'Dead Man's Curve' and that many bikers had been killed there. Two weeks later Frank had fixed my bike. I suggested we take our first ride to 'Dead Man's Curve.'

"You're sure you want to go there?" Frank shook his head.

"Yes, let's take the same route." I was sure.

The smooth and steady engine sound of my blue Suzuki Bandit stirred my longing for freedom, travel and adventure. My bike invited me for another ride and my heart beat faster.

I rode with care, protective of my shoulder. I still felt the occasional pinch of pain. Before every turn I slowed down; I didn't seek speed or thrill. It would take a year to trust myself 100 percent to handle my machine and to lean comfortably into the sharp turns.

We rode along the Pacific Coast. The deep blue ocean, still on the surface, watched silently. Then we turned inland and followed the serpentines into the mountains.

At the stop sign, I came to a standstill and took a deep breath. I felt calm and relieved to ride my Bandit again. Then I opened the throttle to turn left. The old trees spread their shade onto the road, painting abstract patterns onto the asphalt. I did not accelerate but approached 'Dead Man's Curve' slowly. To my surprise, the place that had claimed many lives was bathed in glistening sunlight. We parked our bikes and walked over to the curve.

"It looks so innocent," I said to Frank.

Next to the guard rail I discovered a broken off red reflector. A thick layer of sand covered the spilled engine oil. I kneeled down and took a handful of sand, let it run through my fingers. A chill rushed through me. Frank hugged me, held me tight. Then we got back on our bikes and rode away.

EPILOGUE

October 22, 2010. The four year anniversary of my motorcycle accident was a crisp fall day in Pittsburgh. I had taken the day off to celebrate life, a ritual I had started the first year after the crash. I pulled my new machine, a silver 100 horse power Suzuki Bandit 1250 out of the garage. The weather was on my side; 54 degrees and white puffy clouds floated beneath a clear sky. On the East Coast one never knew at this time of year and soon riding season would be over.

I had returned to Pennsylvania in the spring of 2008. During the months following the accident, I identified the meaning of the unusual sense of intense peace that was so new to me. I realized that I had found what I was looking for and my search was over. Life gained a different quality. It felt as if everything in my everyday reality needed to align itself with what I had experienced while I was out of my body. There was no place for drama or struggle, and everything that didn't come easily needed to fall away.

Consequently, Frank and I did not stay together and went our separate ways. I liked Southern California, a place of beauty, but also fast paced and not as laid back as I had imagined. I found myself working long hours just to pay for the basic costs of living, without being able to save money for travel. Life in Pittsburgh had been good, comfortable and very relaxed. And, of course, I missed all my friends. So I decided to return. I even moved back into the same house, where I had lived before.

I started the machine. The engine sound brought the familiar sense of excitement and adventure. I rode my favorite country roads along farms and green cow pastures into West Virginia. Trees had turned yellow, orange and rust-colored, some already barren and unable to hold on to their leaves.

In Weirton, I pulled into a fuel station. A woman stopped her van at the next pump; her face lit up into the biggest smile. "I love seeing girls doing things they are not supposed to be doing," she said and marked the words with air-quotations. I estimated her around my age, close to her mid-forties. Her long hair was colored raven-black and she had sun-tanned skin. I nodded, returned the smile.

Before getting back onto the main street, I looked up to the sky blue water tower and laughed aloud as I read the inscription 'City of Weirton – Success in Unity.' Countless times I had come down this road and had never seen it. The words 'Success in Unity' felt like a special message to me. Unity is the ultimate goal of all spiritual searches. Unity transcends polarity, which is the experience of our everyday lives, where opposites create one another, good and bad, right and wrong, day and night, and so forth. A world of judgment, struggle and drama. Whereas unity represents the world where everything just is and has the right to exist. There is no judgment about anything and everything is good. A state of enlightenment and complete peace.

Fifteen minutes later I parked my bike next to the Pleasant Valley United Methodist Church and walked to the labyrinth. During my facilitator training, a fellow student mentioned this sacred circle and I began to visit it regularly. The 11-circuit 55-foot stone labyrinth is nestled in between a white stained glass-windowed country church and a forested hill site. Memorial stones for deceased loved ones border the labyrinth's outer circle. The first time I walked it in 2005, I sensed a special connection and had asked permission to place a memorial stone for my dad.

I entered the labyrinth and my mind was calm like the surface of a mountain lake. Aware of my immense peace and clarity, I was grateful that this feeling stayed with me the past four years. There was nothing that needed to be done, just stepping forward, one foot in front of the other and trust.

I walked with ease, inspired by the play of light and shade. Clouds moved in front of the sun, dropping the temperature and casting shadows, then trekked onward and allowed bright rays of sun to reach me without obstruction. I viewed this constant spectacle of change as an outside appearance that didn't affect me. I had tasted the light and know that there is nothing else, just like when we shine light into the shadow, the shadow turns to light.

In the center I stood still. Barking of dogs and ringing of chimes drifted to my ears, and the sun came out again. I closed my eyes and felt as if the inside of my head were a spacious field of gold. I lost my sense of time, opened my eyes and leisurely followed the same path out on which I had come in. With every step I took, I repeated the word 'Yes.' First slowly, only in my mind, then I spoke it aloud. I experimented with different voices, low and deep, stretching the vowel; quick and fast like a determined push, the 'Yes' echoed from the hillside. A lust for life and the insatiable hunger for more rushed through me.

Then I slowed down, became quiet and walked along the outer circle to the opposite side of the labyrinth's entrance. I kneeled and let my hands glide over my dad's memorial stone. Engraved black letters read *In loving memory of our father Karl Brauer.*

Silently I said, "For now I am here. I'll enjoy every moment that I'm alive. And I'll make sure to live a full life."

I stood up and thought about the many times I had moved, and I will, no doubt, do it again. Leaping into a different reality allowed me to grow. The challenges of new beginnings shattered old beliefs and perceptions. Entering foreign terrain revealed parts to me, about myself, that otherwise I would never know.

I smiled, got back onto my machine and continued along the Ohio River.

NOTES:

[1] In 2009 the hedge maze in New Harmony was restored and partly replanted, back to its 'original' Harmonist design. Now it is a hedge labyrinth, rather than a maze.

[2] In 2008 the carpet labyrinth at Grace Cathedral was removed and a new labyrinth was inlaid in stone in the floor.

Acknowledgements

My deepest gratitude goes to all labyrinth builders and visionaries for creating these sacred circles and spiritual transformation power tools for all of us to enjoy. I am grateful for all fellow labyrinth enthusiasts, and the friends at Veriditas and The Labyrinth Society.

I feel privileged and honored to be a madwoman at the *Madwomen in the Attic* writing program at Carlow University in Pittsburgh, Pennsylvania. I am deeply grateful to Nancy Kirkwood, Jan Beatty and the fellow madwomen. Thank you also to the close circle of friends who read the manuscript and gave insightful suggestions.

Special thanks to British labyrinth experts Jeff Saward and Sig Lonegren for reviewing *Girls Don't Ride Motorbikes*.

I am grateful for Mary Hagan Double's creative talent as the designer of the book cover.

Infinite appreciation and love to my parents, Karl and Maria Brauer, my brother, Jörg, and our ancestors.

And of course thank you to you, the reader and fellow seeker. See you on the path.

Lots of love, Dorit

Made in the USA
Monee, IL
03 July 2021

72213394R00125